From Gothic (
Cult TV Th
The Baker and Berman Story

Andrew Llewellyn

A We Belong Dead Presentation

I would like to acknowledge a debt of gratitude to all those who have contributed to the myriad and disparate sources I have drawn upon during my research. Without the meticulous work that has gone before, I would not have been able to have rendered such a (hopefully) thorough record of Baker and Berman's career.

Thanks also to my copy editor Darrell Buxton for identifying those errors in my work that I failed to spot and for helping me arrive at a title for the book, and to Steve Kirkham for helping with the cover layout.

In addition, my appreciation is extended to Eric McNaughton - editor of *We Belong Dead* magazine - who gave me my very first writing assignment a few years back and who has been a valued friend ever since, to Allan Bryce - editor of *Darkside* magazine who has also printed some of my work and given me a great deal of encouragement, to artist Paul Watts for the lovely cover illustration, and to Dawn Dabell for all her valuable advice.

Finally, thank you to my long-suffering wife Melanie who has had to patiently endure having endless passages read to her during the course of the book's writing. At long last she can find peace!

Introduction:

With a publication that has the word 'gothic' in its title, it must surely be appropriate to proceed with a discussion about what the word means, at least within the realms of popular media. When used to describe a cinematic work, it invariably conjures up a general idea in the minds of most movie fans as to what to expect. Following a long tradition of art and literature, the phantasmagorical theatre of 'grand guignol', romantic melodrama and abstract expressionism, gothic films are instantly recognisable via the use of certain archetypes such as locations, character types and visual signifiers. Beyond the literal definition of gothic films as adaptations of 19th century literature or dramas set within that same historical setting, gothic horror itself - derived from such famous novels as Mary Shelley's *Frankenstein* (1818), Bram Stoker's *Dracula* (1897) and the macabre short stories and poems of Edgar Allan Poe (written between 1827 and 1849) - is typified onscreen by the use of such variable elements as wild and desolate, windswept landscapes, stark and lonely, ruined abbeys and ornate and foreboding medieval fortresses within which lie networks of mysterious, hidden passages and dungeons built for torture. The action usually takes place in uncanny, secluded settings such as misty, moonlit graveyards or in the shadows of cobweb-strewn castle corridors,

with heroes and heroines - often plagued by dark family secrets or ancestral curses - endangered by, and pitting their wits against, some malevolent tyrant or supernatural force.

Early examples of gothic horror on celluloid include Robert Wiene's *Das Cabinet des Dr Caligari / The Cabinet of Dr Caligari* (1920) and F W Murnau's *Nosferatu, eine Symphonie des Grauens / Nosferatu, a Symphony of Horror* (1922). The visual styles we now associate with expressionism loom large in both these items: the oddly contorted streets, crooked houses, grotesque characters and painted shadows of *Caligari* perfectly convey a disturbingly distorted physical reality to great effect, and in *Nosferatu* the use of low-key lighting and deep space creates a strong contrast between light and dark that is deeply unnerving. The inventive techniques employed on these two films and the characters displayed within have had a considerable effect on the iconography of cinema that is still felt today, their highly unusual aesthetic helping to define and establish what we now recognise as 'gothic cinema'.

Conrad Veidt in *The Cabinet of Dr Caligari* (1920)

A few years later, the synergy of all these various elements would be streamlined into a more commercial shape when Universal Pictures under Carl Laemmle began their early forays into the form that included the silent classics *The Phantom of the Opera* (1925) starring Lon Chaney Snr and *The Man Who Laughs* (1928) starring *Caligari*'s Conrad Veidt as the disfigured Gwynplaine, a man cursed with a perpetual rictus grin (although this particular picture is arguably not actually a horror film).

Upon the untimely death of Lon Chaney Snr from lung cancer and the introduction of sound to film, Universal went from strength to strength during the 1930s with a succession of black and white gothic horror movies that propagated a fanciful image of remote European hamlets as strange, backward places populated by mad professors, suave vampiric noblemen and torch-bearing villagers prone to rampaging through the streets in pursuit of some fearsome monster. Usually starring - more often than not - the Hungarian actor Bela Lugosi, Englishman Boris Karloff or Lon Chaney Jnr (and with a marvellous additional rotation of supporting actors and occasional leads such as Basil Rathbone, Claude Rains and John Carradine), these movies featured a well-loved variety of supernatural protagonists such as Dracula, Frankenstein's monster, the Invisible Man and the Wolf Man. Over the decades between then and now, the popularity of gothic horror as entertainment has occasionally waned a little but has ultimately endured.

In recent years, films such as *Crimson Peak* (2015), *A Cure for Wellness* (2017) and *The Limehouse Golem* (also 2017); and such television serials as *Penny Dreadful* (2014), *The Alienist* and *The Haunting of Hill House* (both 2018) have proven beyond doubt that the public's hunger for creepy tales of haunted mansions, depraved Victorian serial killers, vampire sects and deranged scientists is as strong now as it ever was. Nowadays - thanks partially to revivalists like Tim Burton - reflections of

gothic iconography are everywhere, almost to a point where it is taken for granted. Comedic television characters such as Morticia Addams (Carolyn Jones) and Lily Munster (Yvonne De Carlo), or larger than life movie icons such as the arch-eye-browed 'Vampira' (Maila Nurmi) and the ample-bosomed, gum-chewing Elvira, Mistress of the Dark (Cassandra Peterson) are 20th century examples of a more tongue-in-cheek, humorous approach where gothic horror meets rock and roll; morbid but highly entertaining characters whose make-up schemes and striking attire have proven to be a huge influence on the fashion industry of today and the inspiration for an entire modern sub-culture.

Back in the mid-1950s, however, Universal had become virtually redundant in the horror stakes, with their once successful formula now tired and lacking in fresh ideas. In 1956, the United Artists feature *The Black Sleep* seemed to serve as a bitter-sweet, cinematic eulogy to a golden era, with a grossly overweight and alcohol-ravaged Lon Chaney Jnr playing alongside a morphine-addicted Bela Lugosi. Cast here in trivial, minor roles and in the dying years of their once magnificent careers, Lugosi and Chaney appear as pitiful shadows of their former selves. *The Black Sleep,* nevertheless, appeared at a rather pertinent juncture, a film with greater relevance than might first be assumed. Just a year later, British company Hammer Films would breath fresh air into

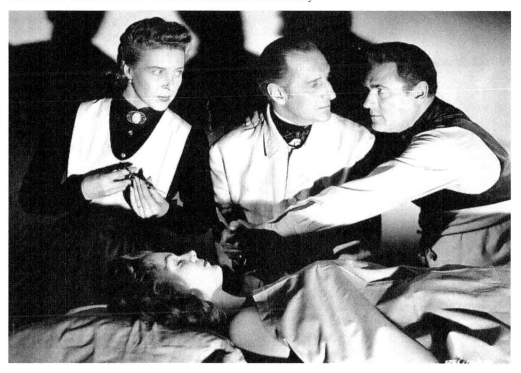

The Black Sleep (1956) - Phyllis Stanley, Basil Rathbone, Herbert Rudley

the gothic-horror sub-genre with their full colour, revolutionary gore-fest (at least by the standards of the day) *The Curse of Frankenstein* (1957). *The Black Sleep*, with much of its action set in a labyrinthine, fully fortified abbey - complete with concealed staircases, a secret laboratory and a dungeon - tells the tale of a mad scientist (Sir Joel Cadman, played by Basil Rathbone) who enlists a condemned prisoner to help him with his terrible experiments on human beings. Thematically similar in many ways to *Curse* - and several of Hammer's future Frankenstein treatments - *Sleep* may have beaten Hammer to the punch if given a bigger budget, a splash of Technicolor and a few buckets of blood. Sadly, it was not to be, and Reginald Le Borg's pedestrian, 'jobbing' approach to directing resulted in a film that is a little too retrospective for its own good, albeit unknowingly so.

From 1957 through to the late sixties, Hammer Films - with their welcome infusion of vivid colour, moral ambiguity, violence and sexuality (often more implied than executed) - would become synonymous with this type of feature and recognised line-leaders in the industry. Generally, when people think of the '50s and '60s in relation to gothic horror, it is either Hammer who immediately spring to mind, with their inspired re-workings of the Dracula, Frankenstein and Mummy

The Curse of Frankenstein (1957)   *The Pit and the Pendulum* (1961)

characters; or American International Pictures, with their excellent and atmospheric succession of Edgar Allan Poe adaptations directed by Roger Corman and starring Vincent Price (commonly referred to as the 'Corman-Poe cycle'). There were, of course, other companies interested in tapping into this new vein of prosperity (Amicus, for instance) and it is here that the subjects of this book, Baker and Berman, and their production company Tempean Films, come in. In 1957, heavily influenced by the huge popularity of Hammer's *Curse of Frankenstein* (and hoping to replicate its success), Baker and Berman took a detour from their usual modus operandi to embark on the production of their very own gothic style horror film, *Blood of the Vampire* (1958), the first in a sequence of similar features to follow from the company. Of course, Baker and Berman were far more than just exponents of gothic horror, and, although a sizeable part of this study will indeed focus on the various Tempean productions that fall within this category and the periods in which they were made, there will also be an examination of their careers as a whole, and the immense body of work attributed to them...

Chapter One:

Formed in 1948, Tempean's initial purpose was to produce short comedy and thriller b-movies suitable for use as supporting features for bigger budget 'head-liners'. During the period, audiences were accustomed to 'double-bills', and a three-hour programme at theatres was the standard. While this was the usual practice, Baker and Berman would find a steady demand for the type of production they were then committed to making, and for roughly a decade this is exactly what they did; releasing an impressive number of lively and fast-paced films that were often staged well enough to look far more expensive than anything their modest budgets should really have allowed (these productions ordinarily took about three weeks to complete, at a cost of between £12,000 and £25,000). However, these types of pictures (of which vast numbers were made, by various companies) were not subject to any special promotion or professional critique, and, widely regarded as nothing more than disposable appetisers made purely to satisfy quota requirements, were easily forgotten over a short space of time. Rather a shame, really, as Tempean were churning out b-movies that were of a far better quality than many being put out by rival companies, films which in retrospect deserved far more attention and appreciation than they got.

From the get-go, Baker and Berman were extremely savvy and knew precisely what they were trying to achieve, with a very good idea of how to achieve it; by assembling a reliable team of competent behind-the-scenes personnel and building up an impressive pool of talented and efficient actors with the ability to work to a tight budget and schedule; Tempean's very own 'repertory company', if you will. The company managed to achieve a great continuity in quality and tone that is not normally associated with films of this nature, thanks in part to the repeat use of certain actors, and of a rotation of directors that included Robert Baker himself. Along with such other regular directors as Charles Saunders, Henry Cass and C Pennington-Richards, Tempean also prospered from the involvement of John Gilling, a prolific and exacting director who would also provide screenplays on many occasions and who would later find himself working extensively with Hammer Films on such movies as *The Plague of the Zombies* (1966) and *The Mummy's Shroud* (1967). Monty Berman also added to this feel of continuity in his role of cinematographer. Berman: 'Because I'm co-producer with Robert I can take far more chances than an ordinary cameraman. I don't have to worry about where my next job is coming from.'

Another factor that made Tempean's b-movies uncommon for the times in which they were made was the use of actual exterior locations to add an extra dimension, rather than just making do with the confines of studio bound interiors and painted backdrops. Despite the problems faced with exterior work (such as having to seek permission from all manner of authorities), shooting on location, if planned correctly, could often work out a lot cheaper than building an array of ambitious sets. Baker: 'Since we would select our locations before production, we would

Baker and Berman reunite, in their later years

make quite sure that they were feasible, weren't going to be too expensive and that the hire cost wasn't going to be too high. We were shooting on locations before it was the popular thing to do. Nowadays if they go on location, they have all sorts of wagons; eating wagons, food wagons, cars or trailers for the stars, and so forth. We had none of that. We just went in two or three cars, and the location manager would go to the nearest café at lunchtime and get some sandwiches and an urn of tea or coffee or something and we would quite often just sit at the kerb, sometimes having our lunch during shooting. We'd never thought of taking a caravan for an actor. We used to go somewhere and go into a pub and hire a couple of rooms so the actors could get changed if they had to. We'd make do on a day-to-day basis. It was planned, but it was planned very economically.'

Robert Sidney Baker was born in London on October 17, 1916. Likewise, Nestor Montague 'Monty' Berman was also born in London, in the Whitechapel district three years earlier on August 16, 1913. Baker was schooled at Tenterden Hall in Middlesex, while Berman's education took place at the University College School in Hampstead. Berman's career in the movie industry began at the age of 17, when he began working as a camera assistant at Twickenham Film Studios in south-west London in 1930. At the time, Twickenham was the largest studio in the UK and operated under the management of Julius Hagen. For many years, Twickenham's main business was the production of 'quota quickies'; features made as cheaply and efficiently as possible for major US studios, who, in a reciprocal arrangement, were required to fund and produce a specified quota of British films per year in order to release their own American pictures onto the UK market. This eventually led to Hagen's desire to release British films in the US, resulting in the gradual cessation of his production of 'quickies'.

It was around this time (1934) that Berman moved on to work at Teddington Studios in Richmond-on-Thames, graduating from camera assistant to camera operator, a development which led to his working alongside the legendary and highly influential film-maker Michael Powell on such items as *Someday* (1935) and *The Edge of the World* (1937). After a short while, Berman once again moved on, leaving Teddington in 1938 to work at Ealing Studios, in the days when they were producing comedies starring Gracie Fields, George Formby and Will Hay. Then, of course, fate intervened. World War II broke out, and the course of his life was changed forever. Drafted into the British Army and attaining the rank of sergeant, Berman was able to continue his craft during the conflict when he was enlisted as a camera operator into the AFPU (army film and photographic unit), whose task was to record military events, often on the field of battle.

Robert Baker, having been a keen amateur director with several prize-winning documentaries under his belt, began his film-making career proper in 1937, when he worked as assistant director on a 20-minute musical affair entitled *A Night in Havana*. Baker first met and befriended Monty Berman when Baker (also a sergeant, in the Royal Artillery) was posted to the deserts of North Africa where he also became involved with the AFPU, later serving as a combat cameraman in Europe. This was no 'soft option', however. The war office required soldiers with professional pre-war experience for this role, and the job was fraught with danger, with over a fifth of AFPU personnel being killed while filming frontline action. Fortunately, Baker and Berman were spared this fate, and once demobilised at the end of the war, the friendship that began during their military service continued in their civilian lives, ultimately turning into a lifelong business relationship borne of their formation of Tempean Films. The two comrade's mutual experience of the desert campaign was later drawn upon in their first 'A' feature, *Sea of Sand* (1958) starring Michael Craig and Richard Attenborough. In the post-war period, Berman worked as a camera operator on such films as *Hue and Cry* (1947; starring Alastair Sim), Powell and Pressburger's *The End of the River* (also 1947) and the macabre psychodrama *Daughter of Darkness* (1948), before Tempean was formed on the goodwill of family and friends.

Regarding the company's origins, Robert Baker made the following recollection in 1995: 'When we got out of the army, we decided that we were going to make our own pictures. We were demobbed at roughly the same time, and we begged, borrowed and stole to get the finance together to make a film called *A Date with a Dream* (1948). That was our first break, as it were, in the movie business. We were naïve at that time, so we used our own money, which we probably would have been forced to do anyway, because, coming out of the army, we had no reputation to fall back on. So, we financed it ourselves; I think the film cost just under £10,000.' Regarding effective distribution, without which all their efforts would have been pointless, Robert Baker had this to say, in 2000: 'We didn't go to a distributor to get a deal to make *A Date with a Dream*, but we showed it to a company called Eros who liked the picture and decided to finance us on subsequent pictures, so then we had a distribution deal with them. We were coming in on budget with presentable pictures and they were happy with them. We must have made twenty or thirty pictures with Eros.' This first feature was made at a now long gone, tiny studio in Kensington called Viking, as well as at various London locations such as the Collins Music Hall in Islington (once a distant memory but recently re-purposed as a live music venue), Brixton Station and the Edgeware Road.

Tempean's board of directors consisted of Baker and Berman themselves, along with Baker's father Morris, and (briefly) their contract director Dicky Leeman, with whom they had originally conceived Tempean. Berman already knew Leeman from when they had both worked on *The Edge of the World*, but during the British Army's retreat from Gazala to Alamein Leeman and Baker's paths crossed, when RAF driver Leeman gave Baker a lift. Leeman departed the company after just one film to work in television variety. From the very beginning, the company operated with admirable guile. In the '40s, it was possible to start up a new enterprise for as little as £100, but Baker and Berman shrewdly decided to finance their venture with the sum of £1000. This effected the potential for more shareholders, with far more units to allocate. Furthermore, the seeking of an alliance with Eros Films Ltd was further evidence of Baker and Berman's considerable business acumen.

Formed post-WWII by former cinema owner brothers Phil and Sydney Hyams, Eros operated by buying up American films to show in the UK and then acquiring British films to use as second or co-features, and for Tempean, this was a perfect fit. Eros were, of course, a well-established distributor long before their association with Tempean, a company that would eventually become leading exhibitors of late '50s cult material such as *Godzilla, King of the Monsters!* (1956), *Womaneater* (1958) and *Grip of the Strangler* (also '58) before folding in 1961. The Hyams brothers - who moved from running movie theatres into film distribution due to a very real fear that one of their London picture-houses might be bombed by the Luftwaffe - are considered by many to be unsung heroes of the British film industry.

Additionally, Baker and Berman adopted the practice of buying or setting up 'loss companies' such as CIPA, Kenilworth, Mid-Century and New World, against which they could write off the company's profits, a crafty but wholly legitimate tax manoeuvre which also allowed them to maintain a production schedule that would be unthinkable to many producers. Tempean's sustained success throughout the fifties can be partly accounted for by these factors, but also by their intrinsic understanding of the operational processes of the National Film Finance Corporation. Baker: 'If you had a film that was successful, and you wanted to borrow money from the NFFC for a new picture, they often asked you to cross-collateralise that successful film with the one you wanted to make. If the new film didn't make any money within a certain time, the NFFC could secure their loan by taking the profits from the successful film to set off against it. You went to a distributor who would give you a distribution contract that covered 75% of the budget. A bank would then advance you money against that contract, leaving a 25% percentage to find in order to finance a picture. What we used to invariably do was to defer our fees, covering a certain amount of that 25%, and the NFFC would put up the rest.'

A Date with a Dream is an earnest but flawed affair that tells a well-worn tale - somewhat reminiscent of a typical MGM Mickey Rooney / Judy Garland production of the '40s - in which a group of would-be stars put on a musical production and, against all the odds, are a success. The picture had autobiographical undertones too, with its tale of plucky ex-servicemen who stage a reunion variety show following their experiences in wartime North Africa. Despite its faults (which are only to be expected

Terry-Thomas and Wally Patch star in *A Date with a Dream* (1948)

in what is essentially a fledgling production) the film has a likeable enthusiasm about its execution, and performances that are earnest and endearing. Additionally, the film's variety routines have a great sense of spontaneity about them that was achieved by using three cameras simultaneously. The item features the comedy dynamics of Len and Bill Lowe, an auspicious debut by British comedy stalwart and well-loved, bumbling clown figure Norman Wisdom (spotted by Berman performing a fill-in comedy routine at the Brighton Hippodrome), a confident appearance by Yorkshire-born future CBS star Jeannie Carson (an eventual recipient of a Hollywood Walk of Fame star, no less) and a typical performance by that gap-toothed portrayer of well-heeled bounder types, Terry-Thomas. This picture, which was not distributed by

Eros (their participation would begin with Tempean's second, much maligned 1949 production *Melody Club*, filmed at Viking Studios and again starring Terry-Thomas), did not make a profit, the blame possibly lying with the apparently inept accountancy of its distributor, Grand National.

These early efforts were not typical of Tempean's later output, and the company would really hit its stride in the '50s, when they garnered a considerable circuit presence and audience fan-base with the initiation of their prolific, staple output of efficient and enjoyable crime thrillers such

Maxwell Reed in *Blackout* (1950)

as *Blackout* (1950); *No Trace* (also 1950); *The Quiet Woman* (1951) and *13 East Street* (1952).These were films that exuded an unmistakeable British flavour, starring an assortment of dependable, home-grown character actors and actresses such as Charles Victor, Derek Bond, Dermot Walsh, Dinah Sheridan and Jane Hylton. Other talents who helped to enrich the company's output included John Horsley, Michael Balfour, Dora Bryan and Thora Hird. These features were also very telling of the times in which they were made, with suspenseful, no-nonsense plots involving the black-market trading of luxury items still hard to come by in the early post-war era, and tales of ordinary people going to extraordinary lengths to survive the enduring, negative effects that wartime austerity had impacted on society.

Going forward, Baker and Berman would prove to be very effective in meeting marketplace demand, which was mostly geared towards thrillers. Of the many second features and co-features made by Tempean in its many guises during the fifties, only a very small number deviated from the crime thriller mould, such as the comedies *Love in Pawn* (1953), *No Smoking* (1955) and *The Reluctant Bride* (also '55), as well as the two musical items mentioned earlier, *A Date with a Dream* and *Melody Club*. Baker: 'The public appetite was in favour of thrillers... You could make a comedy or a thriller. Anything in between was very dubious. It's easy to hook the audience with a thriller, not so easy to hook them on a soft, romantic plot.' Many of Tempean's films of this era were directed (and often written) by John Gilling, whose schedule was often so busy that he resorted to adapting or re-working old 'quota-quickie' scripts and giving them a new spin, and it is safe to say that Gilling was a great asset to Tempean. Many of their best and most effective noir thrillers were made so as a result of his involvement, and Gilling was also exceptionally capable at planning and preparing multiple features simultaneously, an ability vitally important in maintaining Tempean's feverish production rate, which could run to as many as five pictures a year.

Giving the public what they wanted also involved an occasional sprinkling of 'Americanisation', the use of actors out of the United States. Baker: 'They (American actors) gave a lift to British features, plus the different accent helped to make the picture more universal. They knew the camera and consequently their performances were very, very smooth... The result was a bit like a professionally made pull-over compared to a well-meant, hand-knitted job.' This was a strategy that would not only satisfy British audiences by lending a little international sheen to their features but would also give their product transatlantic appeal. The American actors Tempean imported were not exactly A-listers inundated with work, however, being more the types who, at various times, had attained reasonable levels of success as Hollywood b-movie leads, and despite now having their best years behind them, were still famous enough to be both recognisable to UK audiences and capable of drawing a crowd in the USA.

For the sake of convenience and to save valuable time, Tempean acquired its American cast members via negotiations carried out wholly in the UK with Eros and ex-Universal casting director Bob Goldstein. Baker: 'Goldstein came over here and set up a co-production organisation. He was able to get quite big names. We would make a deal together whereby he would supply the actor and a certain amount of the finance and we would supply the rest.' Basically, Baker and Berman would commission a script with an American lead, and then meet with Eros and Goldstein to discuss what US actor to do a deal with, with Goldstein being given a percentage of the American market.

The Big Frame aka The Lost Hours (1952) - Mark Stevens, Jean Kent

The first of these imported stars to make the journey to the UK was the Ohio-born actor Mark Stevens, who appeared in the 1952 British film noir *The Lost Hours* (US title: *The Big Frame*) as Paul Smith, an American WWII pilot who returns to the UK where he had served during the war for a reunion with former RAF comrades, only to find himself framed for a murder he did not commit. Other Tempean pictures in the crime-thriller mode to utilise American actors included: *Three Steps to the Gallows* (1953; US title: *White Fire*) starring Scott Brady and Mary Castle; *The Gilded Cage* (1955) and *Stranger in Town* (1957) both featuring Alex Nicol; *Tiger by the Tail* aka *Cross-Up* (1955) with Larry Parks; *Hour of Decision* (1957) starring Jeff Morrow, and *Kill Me Tomorrow* (also '57) which featured Pat O'Brien.

As a point of interest, *Tiger by the Tail* is notable as being the project with which Larry Parks was given the opportunity to make a film in the more tolerant political climate of the UK, away from the US where his career had been destroyed during the McCarthy Witch-hunt trials of

Larry Parks, star of *Tiger in the Tail* (1955) and *The Jolson Story* (1949)

1950. Parks had worked his way up from bit-part to lead actor during the '40s, culminating in his best-known role, playing Al Jolson in the two films *The Jolson Story* (1946) and *Jolson Sings Again* (1949).

Unfortunately for Parks, it was discovered - during the period of extreme paranoia known in America as the 'second red scare' - that he had once been a member of a Communist Party cell. Subsequently he was summoned to appear before the House Committee on Un-American Activities, and, after giving his testimony, Parks was blacklisted, resulting in the loss of his contract with Columbia Pictures. *Tiger by the Tail* was well received, a tense thriller that made good use of atmospheric London backgrounds and which was justly released on the Odeon circuit. Parks' co-star was the Hollywood-adopted starlet Constance Smith, who was described in the part as 'pert and courageous'. Other Tempean b-movies from this era worthy of mention are *The Frightened Man* (aka *Rosselli and Son*; 1952), *The Voice of Merrill* (aka *Murder Will Out*; also '52) and *Impulse* (1954).

John Gilling's *Frightened Man* stars Charles Victor as Mr Rosselli, a junk dealer who is disappointed when his son Julius (Dermot Walsh) returns home after failing to graduate from Oxford University. Rosselli has been acting as a 'fence' for a gang of Camden town thieves led by Martin Benson as criminal mastermind Alec Stone. Feeling betrayed

The Frightened Man **(1952) - Dermot Walsh**   **Valerie Hobson**

after the gang decide to cut him out of a planned jewel robbery, Rosselli turns them in to the police, not realising that his son Julius has become embroiled with the gang, dashing any hopes he ever had of his progeny reaching a higher station in life than his own. The feature ends tragically at the climax of a terrific rooftop chase sequence expertly filmed by Gilling. By and large, the film has some interesting moments, including one scene which reflects the social attitudes of the day; Julius is in Rosselli's store, and is seen to behave negatively towards his father's assistant Cornelius (Michael Ward), who, by his very demeanour, is patently homosexual.

Also directed by Gilling (from a screenplay written by himself in collaboration with Gerald Landeau and Terence Austin), *The Voice of Merrill* is a tense mystery drama that benefits considerably from the presence of Valerie Hobson, an actress of some repute. Having starred in classics such as *Bride of Frankenstein* (1935) and *Great Expectations* (1946), Hobson brings an air of class and elegance to the item in her role of Alycia, the wife of an arrogant playwright named Jonathan Roach (James Robertson-Justice). The film's complicated plot involves the murder of a female blackmailer and the attempts by investigating police officer Inspector Thornton (Garry Marsh) to work out which of three suspects is responsible. Meanwhile, Alycia, tired of her loveless marriage, begins an affair with another writer (Edward Underdown as Hugh Allen, one of the suspects) and is soon dreaming up ways to dispose of her husband. The titular 'Voice of Merrill' alludes to a radio serial that the obnoxious Roach has written, and which Alycia's lover somehow ends up narrating, the broadcasts serving as a highly unusual plot device wherein pertinent facts regarding the identity of the blackmailer's killer are gradually revealed. Eros recognised that this item was unusually sophisticated and stylish for a b-movie and elevated its status to that of a co-feature, and on release *The Voice of Merrill* sometimes even played as the main feature on a double bill. It seems that Tempean were often

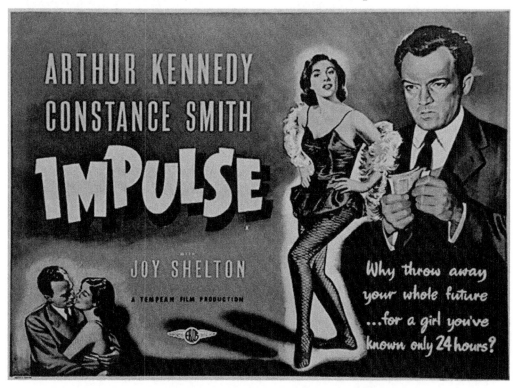

unaware of just how good some of their output actually was.

Impulse is also another extremely good picture that wears its 'noir' influences firmly on its sleeve. Arthur Kennedy - *Rancho Notorious* (1952), *A Summer Place* (1959) - plays Alan Curtis, an American lawyer living in Britain who is suffering a bit of an existential crisis in which the humdrum nature of his daily routine is driving him to distraction and misery. As such, the bored Curtis is easily lured into the seedy world of London night-life by alluring nightclub singer and femme-fatale Lila (*Tiger by the Tail*'s Constance Smith, once again), soon becoming involved in the criminal activities of her club-owner boss. The film has a terrific atmosphere of big city danger and was directed by Cy Endfield of *Mysterious Island* (1961) and *Zulu* (1964) fame. At the time of *Impulse*, Cy Endfield was blacklisted (just as Larry Parks was) by the HUAC, so Tempean fabricated a fictitious entity by the name of Charles de Lautour - in fact, a pseudonym for Endfield - to ensure that the movie could be distributed in America.

In 1955, Tempean found themselves facing fresh challenges. The ever-reliable director/writer John Gilling suddenly became less available due to his commitments to bigger companies such as Warwick Films, and his last script for Baker and Berman was for the 1956 thriller

Constance Smith, star of Impulse (1955)

Bond of Fear, directed by Henry Cass. Never content to rest on their laurels, Baker and Berman began to consider new ideas. Their old colleague Dicky Leeman had already achieved great success as the producer of the BBC's panel show '*What's My Line?*', and now Baker and Berman began to consider the benefits of moving into television themselves, something they would eventually do with a great degree of success in the '60s and '70s when they simply transferred their proven low-budget skills to a different medium. This train of thought was exemplified by their decision to develop a series of movies featuring a private detective called 'Duke' Martin, a character played by Tom

Conway in the films *Barbados Quest* (1955) and *Breakaway* (1956) that they tentatively hoped might make the transition to the small screen, although this was ultimately not the case.

By the time Baker and Berman were shooting *Blind Spot* - a re-make of the 1950 film *Blackout* that features an early appearance by Michael Caine - for Butcher's Film Service (another British film company

Tom Conway (as 'Duke' Martin) and Honor Blackman in *Breakaway* (1956)

specialising in the production and distribution of low-budget fare) they had become acutely aware that the market for b-movies was rapidly dwindling and felt that they were now simply 'treading water'. With new media and formats emerging, a change was needed, and Bob Baker told the press that there were plans to shoot in colour, and perhaps even use CinemaScope. Influenced by the evident popularity of science-fiction and the new sensation of 'Hammer Horror', Tempean were now ready to move into making pictures of a very different nature to those for which they were thus far known, a transition that would take them into the realms of the 'A' feature and the X-certificate. In 1958 they not only bought up the rights to '*The Trollenberg Terror*' - a six-part science-fiction series broadcast by the ITV television network in late '56 /early '57 - with the intention of making their own feature length version of the serial, but also set to work on the first of their gothic horror outings, *Blood of the Vampire...*

Chapter Two:

'The most loathsome scourge ever to afflict this earth was that of the vampire. Nourishing itself on warm living blood, the only known method of ending a vampire's reign of terror was to drive a wooden stake through its heart.'

From the moment that *Blood of the Vampire* begins, with its brief prologue that shows the mountain-top staking of a mysterious shrouded body and the subsequent stabbing to death of a gravedigger, there can be no doubt whatsoever as to what Baker and Berman's intentions were with the picture. As the preceding italicized words, boldly emblazoned on-screen in jagged, yellow letters at the film's opening testify, this was unashamedly a Hammer rip-off. Tempean even went as far as to procure the services of regular Hammer scribe Jimmy Sangster to help attach a modicum of that special 'Hammer flavour' to the feature; those formulaic, tried and tested elements that Sangster had perfected and used before on *X the Unknown* (1956) and *The Curse of Frankenstein* (1957) and which he would use again here and on future projects.

   It was, perhaps, still a little early for anyone to be able to accurately pin-point the absolute essence of what made Hammer such a success, but Tempean's approach and use of Sangster worked reasonably well. Well enough, in fact, that despite suffering from the odd poorly rendered matte background or a ropey looking prop here and there, *Blood of the Vampire* - which was filmed at Twickenham - has, on occasion, been

mistaken for a Hammer film by those without the discerning sense of scrutiny required to tell the difference. Baker: 'I make no bones about it, we set out to follow Hammer's formula, it was successful for them and it was successful for us... as a writer, Sangster was the "king of horrors". If I went to a distributor and said, "I have a Jimmy Sangster horror picture" they would be interested, no question about that.'

Of course, even with the right personnel on board, there was always the money side of things to take care of. Concerned

Jimmy Sangster

that their new project might suffer from the NFFC's policy for 'cross collateralisation' (the minutiae of which is outlined in the previous chapter), Baker and Berman set up another temporary company, which in this case was named 'Artistes Alliance'. Fortunately for these short-

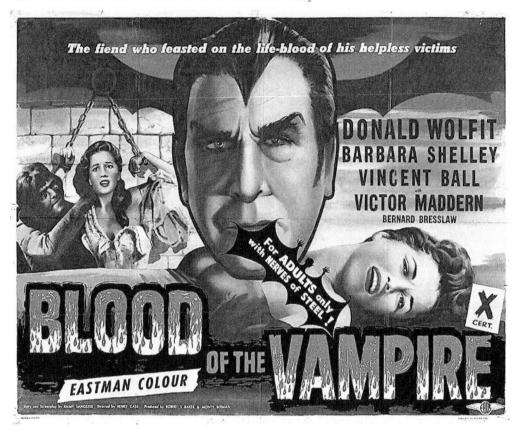

term deals, Tempean's UK distribution deal with Eros was completely transferrable, and in conjunction with added financial support in the USA from Universal-International, *Blood of the Vampire* acquired A-movie status, which allowed for it to be shot over a slightly more generous four-week schedule and, more importantly, in glorious full colour (Eastmancolor, to be exact). Oddly, despite Sangster's involvement and the obvious intent by Tempean to adopt the 'Hammer horror' style, Universal-International's approach in promoting the picture stateside was rather unusual, with poster subtitles such as 'from the pages of science fiction's most shocking tale' and mentions of 'the strange experiments of Dr Callistratus' giving transatlantic movie-goers a somewhat skewed impression of the film's flavour. UK 'quads', however, left no doubt in people's minds whatsoever with sensational blurbs like 'no woman is safe from the most frightening fiend in the history of horror' and 'the fiend who feasted on the life-blood of his helpless victims'.

The film's events begin in Transylvania, 1874; After the staking and attempted burial of an unknown individual, a deformed and repulsive hunch-backed creature by the name of 'Carl' kills the gravedigger, steals the corpse and arranges a heart transplant to be performed on the stolen body, before murdering the unfortunate, drunken surgeon he has procured for the purpose in an unflinchingly brutal manner. Six years pass, and the drama moves to a courtroom in the hamlet of Carlstadt (represented here by a model set that looks suspiciously like one previously used to represent Shakespeare's Globe theatre in 1944's *Henry V*), where Bavarian physician Dr John Pierre (Vincent Ball) is on trial, charged with murder by medical malpractice after his attempt to perform an emergency blood transfusion (a procedure not yet successfully executed) results in the death of a patient. Pierre urges the judge at his trial (John Le Mesurier) to contact a certain 'Professor Bernhardt Meinster of Geneva' who, he says, will vouch for him and confirm that his actions were justified. Unfortunately for Pierre, the judge informs him that he has already written to the Professor, who has inexplicably responded claiming to have never even heard of the accused.

Convicted and sentenced to serve life imprisonment in a penal colony, Pierre is taken to a crowded cell inhabited by a motley assortment of miscreants, where he is visited briefly by his fiancée Madeleine before having to fight off a hulking sneak thief played by a young Bernard Bresslaw. When a horse-drawn Black Maria duly arrives (driven by the murderous Carl) to take Pierre away, the doctor is surprised to discover that his expected fate of a torturous life of penal servitude is not to be, as he is taken instead to a prison for the criminally insane run by a Dr Callistratus. It transpires that the whole situation has been orchestrated, with the revelation that Professor Meinster never received the judge's letter at all, as it was intercepted by a member of the prison commission named Auron (Bryan Coleman), who is on the payroll of Callistratus. Just as in Reginald Le Borg's *The Black* Sleep, where Herbert Rudley (as Dr Gordon Ramsay) is wrongly imprisoned, sentenced to death and then freed as part of the machinations of Basil Rathbone's Sir Joel Cadman (who requires his expertise), Pierre has similarly been 'head-hunted' in a highly deceptive manner, for reasons that soon become clear.

The film's title is a little misleading. The 'vampire' of the piece is not some supernatural fiend that rises from its mouldering grave at the setting of the sun to wander the night in search of its victims, it is Dr Callistratus himself, a mere mortal afflicted with a life-threatening disorder that can only be neutralised by regular transfusions of blood.

This is, of course, the mysterious, shrouded figure staked in Transylvania at the beginning of the film. Believed to be a vampire by the locals and dealt with accordingly, Callistratus has somehow been brought back to life via the heart transplant arranged by Carl. In due course, Pierre discovers the reason for his transfer to the asylum; He is needed to assist Callistratus with his research into blood-typing (essential for successful transfusions, with the asylum being merely a 'front' so that Callistratus and his servant Carl can acquire a regular supply of fresh subjects for their terrible experiments).

In casting for the movie, performers were drawn from the considerable list of those that had appeared in previous Tempean pictures, along with several new faces who would here make their debut for the company. The same year, Baker and Berman produced the BAFTA nominated *Sea of Sand* aka *Desert Patrol*, an actioner set in the deserts of North Africa that tells the story of a mission by the Long-Range Desert Group to destroy a German fuel dump located deep behind enemy lines, on the eve of the battle of El Alamein. Reflecting a little of Baker and Berman's own wartime experience, the film was imbued with a great deal of factual accuracy due to the technical advice of real life former LRDG intelligence officer Bill Kennedy Shaw. Australian actor Vincent Ball played the supporting role of 'Sergeant Nesbitt' in the feature, and it was this capable performance that led to his being cast in the far more substantial

Vincent Ball and John Gregson in Tempean's war-time drama *Sea of Sand* (1958)

Victor Maddern, without make-up!

part of Dr John Pierre. The villainous hunchback - ostensibly a secondary character that even so managed to feature heavily in the movie's promotional material - is portrayed by Victor Maddern, an Essex-born actor best known for playing military types and petty criminals. A familiar face in the landscape of post-war British cinema, Maddern is rendered virtually unrecognisable in the part of 'Carl', his features concealed beneath his character's crudely wrought latex make-up and black fright wig (an unimpressive effort by make-up artist Jimmy Evans of applications which apparently caused Maddern to suffer headaches). For Callistratus - a morally objectionable character who cares little about where or who he gets his blood from - Tempean opted to use Donald Wolfit, a theatre actor of some repute who, with his distinctive eyebrows, just happened to be reminiscent of a heavier set Bela Lugosi, and whose

Callistratus (Donald Wolfit) and his hunchback servant 'Carl' (Victor Maddern)

fee would not break the bank.
Wolfit, who was honoured with
a knighthood in 1957, had been
an active stage performer from
as early as 1924, a regular at the
Old Vic theatre and a thespian
proper whose speciality was
Shakespearean roles.

As could be expected with a
trained actor of such gravitas
and experience, Wolfit
would need considerable
'dumbing down' by *Blood of the
Vampire*'s director, Henry
Cass. A former stage actor
himself and former artistic
director of the Old Vic, Cass
would need to employ a great
deal of tact and sensitivity to
prevent Wolfit from being

The young Donald Wolfit as Hamlet in 1936

overly theatrical. A director previously used by Tempean on the film
Breakaway (1955), Cass was known for his strong instinct for
comedy but was equally adept at horror. Cass, in *Kinematograph
Weekly*: 'If you succeed in scaring the girls in the audience into the arms
of their boyfriends, then you have done your job well.' Robert Baker
added: 'It's so easy to make horror films cheap and nasty, but that is a
short-term policy. Horror, in itself, is not good enough. You've still got to
have a good story, you've still got to make a good motion picture.'

Pierre's fiancée Madeleine - who (after discovering that her beau is the
subject of a conspiracy) infiltrates the asylum under the guise of a
housekeeper, in order to free him - is played by Barbara Shelley, who
was soon to find herself rightly considered the number one female star of
'Hammer Horror'. Widely admired and even revered by modern day fans
of vintage horror movies, Shelley was, at this point in her career, still
relatively unknown, although she had already starred in a handful of
notable cult items such as *Cat Girl* (1957) for Insignia productions and
The Camp on Blood Island (1958) for Hammer. Once cast, the actress
was rather pleased to find herself working alongside Wolfit on the
picture; Shelley: 'When I was six my father took me to the Colosseum to

see Donald Wolfit in *The Merchant of Venice*. That was my introduction to the theatre, that's when I fell in love with it. Anyway, to work with Donald after all those years - well... it was a tremendous experience.'

The music for the film was written and directed by Stanley Black, a jazz pianist and bandleader of great repute who, in the post-war years, was known primarily for being the conductor of the BBC Dance Orchestra in the '40s and a successful recording artist on the Decca label throughout the '50s, before being appointed music director at Elstree Studios in 1958, a position that led to an incredible industry career during which he composed and arranged the music for dozens of film productions.

Returning to the plot, the cruelty of the regime Callistratus has built around himself in his quest for vitality is highlighted early on. As Dr Pierre (still unaware of his destiny) is working in the prison / asylum yard as instructed, a guard is more than prepared to set a vicious Dobermann on a prisoner who has collapsed. Too ill to work, the emaciated inmate is only saved from the jaws of death by the sudden arrival by coach of Callistratus, an event that serves as a welcome distraction. Once Pierre is made privy to the true nature of the institute and the work that he is to be forced into doing there, it is not long before he grows uncomfortable with the exploitation and cruel use of its many inmates and wants out. Once his fiancée infiltrates the prison the suspense is ramped up considerably.

Trusted by Callistratus, Madeleine's undercover mission is put in great peril when she is seen by Auron, who recognises her from an earlier part of the film when she is making enquiries into Professor Meinster's failed acknowledgement of Pierre. Rather than reveal who she is, Auron follows Madeleine to her room with the intent of brutally raping her. Luckily for Madeleine, the hunchback Carl has fallen in love with her and things do not end very well for Auron.

Eventually Callistratus discovers Madeleine's real purpose and chains her to the wall of his laboratory. Pierre attempts to rescue her but is captured and is likewise tethered, before Callistratus instructs his servant Carl to strap Madeleine to an operating table. The smitten creature refuses and Callistratus shoots him for his disobedience, before strapping her down himself.

The evil doctor now intends to transfuse Madeleine's blood into the legless, one-armed Kurt (William Devlin), a fellow prisoner of Pierre's who was supposed to have been killed by the Dobermann guard dogs during an escape attempt earlier in the movie, but who, now virtually nothing more than a torso, has been kept alive for further torments. As Kurt is stretchered in to the laboratory, Jimmy Sangster's penchant for a little black humour is demonstrated when Callistratus says 'Kurt doesn't talk, he doesn't even move about. He just stays where he is without complaining, don't you, Kurt?' As Callistratus proceeds, Pierre urges

Kurt to 'resist' and the unfortunate wretch grips the doctor's arm. As the pair struggle, they move close enough to Pierre for him to knock Callistratus unconscious and free himself, as Kurt finally and mercifully expires from the exertion. Pierre frees Madeleine and takes Callistratus hostage, and the couple bargain their way past the prison guards to freedom. Callistratus does not escape punishment, either. Though shot and mortally wounded, Carl has somehow clung to life, and in a last

defiant act before he is shot by the guards, the hunchback frees the Dobermanns and they attack Callistratus, tearing him to shreds, a deserved fate that strongly recalls the one suffered by Count Zaroff in RKO's pre-code thriller *The Most Dangerous Game* (1932).

Blood of the Vampire's UK premiere took place in London on August 26, 1958, but its international release schedule was a drawn out and staggered affair. Despite getting its US opening - on a double-bill with Universal's *Monster on the Campus* - just a few months later in the October of that year, it took some considerable time before it was released in certain other countries (1966 for Spain, for instance, and, in the case of Sweden, as late as '69). Having now fully embraced a deliberate X-certificate path, this picture was Tempean's first - of four - to have a special 'continental' edit. Baker and Berman's four 'continental' films - which will be discussed in more detail later - were alternate cuts to those released in Britain and the USA, versions which either included the restoration of scenes that had been excised completely or shortened by the British Board of Film Censors (as the organisation was then known) prior to UK release (as with *Blood of the Vampire* and 1961's *The Hellfire Club*) or contained specially re-shot scenes with added nudity, as was the case with 1959's *Jack the Ripper* and *The Flesh and the Fiends* (1960). This was a new and unique approach - taken with the more liberal European market in mind - that would help distributors sell the film more easily, and for a better price. For the UK, Baker and Berman were more than happy to stick to the guidelines of the BBFC, with whom they had so far had an amicable relationship, but who would soon enough have plenty to say about this and their next few productions.

Overall, the critical response to *Blood of the Vampire* in the US was quite favourable. Charles Stinson of *The Los Angeles Times* wrote, 'it is gratifying to be able to turn in an on the whole good report on the film. It is intelligently scripted and well-acted by its British performers', while Jack Moffitt of *The Hollywood Reporter* wrote that 'the feature rates more serious audience attention than most of the contemporary rash of domestic horror films. Direction by Cass is brisk enough to keep yawning from being contagious to the audience.' In the UK, the reaction was a much more mixed bag. Released a few months after the May 7 debut of the far superior *Dracula*, the film could only shrink in stature when displayed next to Hammer's classic shocker on London's giant billboards. Some reviews were positive, and *Picturegoer* said that 'Horror may be big box office business: the trouble is, it starts to be a big bore, too. Here the gory business is redeemed by Donald Wolfit, who plays with a gusto that may not be high art but is certainly highly entertaining... Handsomely mounted in blood-spattered Eastmancolor, the film has plenty of gruesome effects.' On the other hand, The *Monthly Film Bulletin* recognised the item for what it was when it stated that 'This essay in hokum has provided the producers with the chance to incorporate every trick of the macabre and the horrific they can legitimately introduce'. The biggest stumbling block for many with the film was its attempt to provide a rationale for human resurrection via the application of an implausible pseudoscience. Tempean were not too worried. Baker: 'We never paid any attention to critics. They had their own tastes and to some extent they were trying to impose those on the public. The trade papers were slightly different; they guided exhibitors to what films would or would not sell to the public. But nothing said by the so-called mainstream critics mattered, not to this sort of film anyway.'

Chapter Three:

'There are many galaxies besides ours. Who knows what is happening millions of miles out in space? Perhaps the world that these creatures inhabit is coming to an end; perhaps they need to find somewhere else to live...' - Professor Crevett

The Trollenberg Terror (1958; US title: *The Crawling Eye*) was the last ever motion picture to be made at Southall Studios, and is quite possibly the only one made there that today's fans of cult horror and science-fiction cinema might even have heard of. A production facility originally constructed in 1924 on the site of a former aircraft hangar in Middlesex, West London, Southall began its output in 1928 with the silent movie *Two Little Drummer Boys*. From then on, the studio underwent several changes of name (Kingsway General Films Ltd; Britone Sound Studios; Metropolitan Film Studios) and operated sporadically up to the point when it was destroyed by fire on 29th October 1936. The studio was then rebuilt - complete with three stages of varying but modest dimensions - but not properly utilised until 1946, when Sydney Box (who owned

Twickenham and Riverside Studios at the time) acquired it.

Southall then became a hive of activity, being used by various companies, with examples of projects produced within its walls (many directed by Val Guest) including a couple of family movies that featured the exploits of Richmal Crompton's schoolboy tearaway William Brown (*Just William's Luck* and *William Comes to Town* aka *William at the Circus* - both 1948) and Hammer's cheerful and lively comedy *Life with the Lyons* (1954). It was here also that the 26 episodes that make up the television serial *Colonel March of the Yard* (starring Boris Karloff) were made, between 1952 and '54. By this time Southall was in considerable financial difficulty, and this popular series - which counted among its many guest stars such future famous faces as Adrienne Corri, Christopher Lee and Anthony Newley - was helping to keep the studio afloat. Tempean had used the facility on many occasions during the '50s, having filmed *Three Steps to the Gallows* (1953), *The Reluctant Bride* (1955) and *Kill Me Tomorrow* (1957) there, and when Baker and Berman took *The Trollenberg Terror* to its soundstages, Southall's complete collapse was already just a matter of time...

As with *Blood of the Vampire*, Jimmy Sangster was called upon to write the screenplay for *The Trollenberg Terror,* his task; to condense the content of Peter Key's teleplay for ITV's original six-part serial into a script suitable for an 80-minute motion picture. For even a screen-writer as adept as Sangster, the job of having to drastically reduce the running time permitted to tell the tale would present its challenges, and the finished production does indeed have several noticeable loose ends, jarring plot-holes and unfathomable jumps in continuity. Nevertheless, Sangster's heavy truncation of the source narrative does imbue the feature with a fast paced, 'no-nonsense' energy, and Tempean - encouraged by the recent success of other television-to-film adaptations of a similar flavour - were quietly optimistic. Baker: 'Jimmy had done this sort of thing before, and we knew he could do a good job. Don't forget, the *Quatermass* films started out on television too and lost very little in the translation to the big screen.'

At a fictional mountain resort in Switzerland, mysterious events have been occurring. Following a series of disturbing incidents where mountaineers have either disappeared without trace or been found decapitated while attempting to scale 'Trollenberg peak', the locals attribute the horrific fatalities to 'evil spirits' they are certain inhabit the area, a notion reinforced by the sighting of a mysterious cloud hovering

stationary on the mountain's south face, inside which they believe the malignant entities may live. A United Nations operative by the name of Alan Brooks (Forrest Tucker) travels to the area after receiving a letter from a Professor Crevett (Warren Mitchell) requesting his urgent assistance. Crevett is an old friend and colleague of Brooks who now works in a government-funded observatory situated at the mountain-top.

On his train journey, Brooks encounters Geneva-bound sisters Anne and Sarah Pilgrim, whose compartment he shares. One of the sisters (Anne, a stage mind-reader) inexplicably faints as they near Mount Trollenberg, and upon recovering consciousness she has a sudden, powerful compulsion that makes her insist that she and her sister must alight the train at the next stop. After securing lodgings at the 'Europa' hotel and settling in, Brooks decides to visit the observatory and shares the cable-car to his destination with two mountaineers who are on their way to a base-camp lodge on the Trollenberg. At the observatory, Brett is reunited with his old friend Professor Crevett - a cardboard cut-out scientist with a stereotypical comedy German accent - who tells Brett that he has scanned the strange cloud hovering on the mountain and found it to be radioactive. The Professor then suggests a possible link between the recent deaths in the area and previous fatalities that occurred three years earlier in the Andes while he and Brooks were working there together.

The film's leading man Forrest Tucker and his co-star, the beautiful Janet Munro

Later that evening, Brooks returns to the Europa accompanied by Crevett, where Anne (Janet Munro) has offered to give a demonstration of her mind-reading abilities to her fellow guests. While doing so, Anne has a psychic vision of events unfolding at the base-camp lodge on the mountain involving the two men with whom Brooks had earlier shared the cable-car. During this spectacle, Anne 'sees' one of the men (Andrew Faulds as 'Brett') appear to fall under the mental control of some unseen power. Before fainting, she finally witnesses Brett leave his sleeping companion Dewhurst (Stuart Saunders) to go outside, as the weird cloud moves down the mountain and surrounds the lodge. Brooks senses something is not right and attempts to contact the lodge, to no avail. A rescue team is sent out to try to find the two men, but it soon becomes apparent that Brett is no longer in control of his own actions and is on a homicidal rampage, his end goal to kill Anne, whose psychic powers have seemingly been detected as a threat by whatever strange force is inhabiting the mountain.

The hut is reached and found to be inexplicably frozen solid from within, and Dewhurst's headless corpse is discovered under his bed. Leaving the lodge, one of the rescuers finds a rucksack with a severed head inside, before being attacked and slaughtered by Brett on the precipice, as indeed, is a second member of the team. Brett then finds his way to the hotel and attacks Anne. Luckily, the men are at hand to

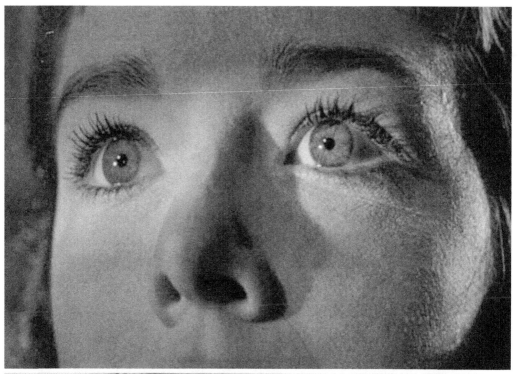

subdue Brett, and on injuring him during the struggle they notice that a wound on his head does not bleed, leading Brooks (recalling his experiences in the Andes) to suspect that Brett is, in fact, dead and an automaton. Brett is sedated and confined to a room, but soon escapes and, curved blade in hand, goes after Anne once more, before being shot by Brooks.

The radioactive cloud suddenly begins to drift down the mountain towards Europa, so the group decide to retreat to Crevett's observatory, which is heavily fortified and made from reinforced concrete. Before they can make their way up the mountain by cable-car, Brooks returns to the resort to locate a missing child and the mist arrives, bringing with it a giant, multi-tentacled monster with a single eye that smashes its way into the hotel. Brooks and the child evade the creature and hastily return to

Crevett (Warren Mitchell), Sarah (Jennifer Jayne) and Alan (Forrest Tucker) in Crevett's lab

the cable-car, narrowly escaping the freezing cloud that pursues it. Once at the observatory, the group arrive at the conclusion that alien beings are using the mountain as a launch base for an all-out invasion of Earth, killing climbers and re-animating some of them to use in further attacks, and it is here that they must make a stand against the monsters, who soon converge on the building.

Helmed by Quentin Lawrence (who also directed the television version), *The Trollenberg Terror* suffers from its obvious budgetary restraints. The mountainous area in which the action takes place is evoked with the use of stock footage of the Alps which matches up poorly with the aesthetic of the interiors and exteriors filmed at Southall. At the very beginning of the film, a pre-credits scene shows two mountaineers witness a climbing companion plummet from a higher point, and as they struggle to pull 'Jim' up, the ledge on which they are perched sounds decidedly hollow. The set design is lacklustre, with Dr Crevett's sparsely equipped observatory - supposedly a state-of-the-art installation - showing all the signs of a scientific facility in dire need of funding, despite the doctor's proud announcement that 'the government gives me as much money as I want'. Jimmy Sangster: 'Most of the movie took place up a mountain in Switzerland and I didn't get to go on location. Come to think of it, I don't think anyone else did either. Tempean was a bit like Hammer when it came to spending money. They probably shot their films in the local gravel pit painted white.' Les Bowie's special effects are unusually below-par, too. Robert Baker: 'On the whole the effects were a let-down. I remember the alien cloud was created using cotton wool (nailed onto a photograph and filmed, according to Bowie himself), and on-screen it looked like... cotton wool. For the most part we focused the action on the characters, not the effects.' The appearance of the aliens themselves also left a lot to be desired, at least initially. Time has perhaps decided otherwise.

The opening credits are perfectly decent, though. Steeped in a timely, minimalist tradition established by Saul Bass on *The Man with the Golden Arm* (1955) and taken to its absolute zenith on *Psycho* (1960), the use of thick white lines on a black background in the sequence creates a graphic tension, and Stanley Black's theme music is brisk and dynamic, with a nice sprinkling of those eerie, theremin driven motifs that seem to evoke a sense of otherworldly strangeness so well. Apart from Quentin Lawrence, whose track record up to this point had been in television - he would later go on to direct Hammer's festively-tinged

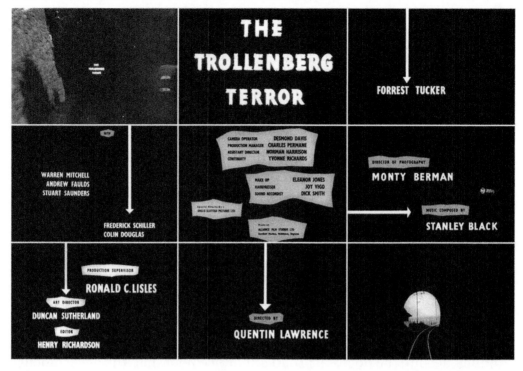

Cash on Demand (1962) and their war film *The Secret of Blood Island* (1964), amongst others - Laurence Payne, another veteran of the Bristol Old Vic theatre company also made the transfer from the tv serial to the film. Many fans of '70s horror will recognise Payne from his portrayal of the Serbian schoolmaster (and cuckolded husband) Albert Müller from Hammer's *Vampire Circus* (1972), but in *The Trollenberg Terror* he plays Philip Truscott, a cynical investigative reporter who mostly has little to do other than make the occasional sarcastic comment (although he does feature prominently in the final battle against the tentacled aliens, complete with 'Molotov cocktails').

Fulfilling the role of Tempean's 'token American' this time around was Forrest Tucker, an Indiana-born actor whose career in entertainment began in vaudeville, when he spent several of his teenage years performing at the Old Gaiety Burlesque Theater in Washington, DC. After moving to California in the late '30s, Tucker's rugged looks and considerable height of six feet five inches led to a contract with Columbia and appearances in dozens of features, mostly Westerns and action films, throughout the '40s. In 1948 Tucker left Columbia and signed with Republic, and it was this new contract that led to Tucker working in the UK on a couple of co-productions. Firstly, Tucker starred in the two features *Laughing Anne* (1953) for Herbert Wilcox Productions (as

Imperadio) and *Trouble in the Glen* (1954) for Everest Pictures. Then, Tucker was cast in the Hammer picture *Break in the Circle* (1955), leading to a major follow-up role for the company as the lead in *The Abominable Snowman* (1957) alongside Peter Cushing. At the time that Tucker appeared in *Trollenberg* his career seemed to be floundering, but he would eventually have a renaissance of sorts in the mid-sixties when he starred in the highly syndicated American television satirical comedy *F Troop*, playing Cavalry Sergeant Morgan O'Rourke, a sort of Wild West frontier version of 'Sgt Bilko'.

In the part of Professor Crevett, Warren Mitchell forgoes his exceptional acting ability (he twice received the Laurence Olivier Award) to deliver a parodic performance. Now well-known in the UK for playing the bigoted cockney 'Alf Garnett' in Johnny Speight's BBC television situation comedy *Till Death Us Do Part* (and its many sequels), Mitchell was not the original choice to play Crevett, and he himself was not even that enamoured with the role, considering it as merely a means to an end. Mitchell: 'They had cast Anton Diffring in the role and at the last minute he decided to go on holiday. My agent told them I was free and could do the accent, so I got the part without even an interview. I did it purely for the money, they paid me enough to put a deposit down on a house and that's exactly what I did. The film was absolute bollocks.'

Janet Munro's portrayal of Anne Pilgrim shows great promise in the early part of *Trollenberg*, when her psychic powers cause she and her sister to travel to the very epicentre of the alien activity, but her role is soon reduced to that of 'damsel in distress'. Genre-wise, the striking actress is probably best remembered for playing 'Jeannie Craig' in British Lion's *The Day the Earth Caught Fire* (1961) but she also starred in several films for Disney - including *Swiss Family Robinson* (1960) - and was BAFTA nominated for her role in the morality tale *Life for Ruth* (1962). Sadly, Munro passed away in 1972 from a heart condition, aged just 38 - leaving her husband (the actor Ian Hendry) a bereft widower who would spend the remainder of his life struggling with alcohol.

Produced a little prior to *Blood of the Vampire*, *The Trollenberg Terror* was released on a double-bill with various pictures, which included a foreign smut-fest titled *Call Girls* and the more appropriate *The Strange World of Planet X* (aka *Cosmic Monsters*, USA). Despite its numerous flaws, the film was well-received; successful enough on both sides of the Atlantic, in fact, to provide a financial springboard for Baker and Berman to embark on their planned gothic adventure. There was also very little in the item to concern the BBFC, with much of the violence either implied or alluded to.

In more recent times, the film's impact on the generations born since its release (and the mark it has left on popular culture) have become quietly apparent. John Carpenter once remarked that the picture was a partial inspiration for his 1980 film *The Fog*, and in 1986, the shape-shifting, titular monster of Stephen King's novel '*It*' manifests itself at one juncture of the book in the form of a 'crawling eye'. In 1975, 'Dragon's Domain' - the 23th episode of the television series *Space: 1999*'s first season - featured a terrifying creature possessing a single, glowing and baleful eye, the design of which must surely have been influenced by the tentacled monstrosities of *Trollenberg*. Additionally, in 1999 the punk band The Misfits included a track entitled 'Crawling Eye' on their album 'Famous Monsters', complete with plot-related lyrics...

Chapter Four:

'You drove my boy to suicide... Like some foul, malignant virus, you and your kind contaminate the gutters you inhabit, the very air you breathe! Nobody's safe... I've been sweeping the streets, looking for you, Mary Clarke...' - Sir David Rogers

In the early hours of August 31, 1888, a gruesome discovery was made. At what was then known as Buck's Row in the impoverished London district of Whitechapel, the body of 43-year-old prostitute Mary Ann Nichols was found, her throat slit twice from left to right and a series of incisions and cuts made to her torso, including a deep and jagged wound in her abdomen. Nichols' death was the first of several that became known as the 'canonical five', a sequence of bloody murders committed that year that are now widely considered to have been carried out by the same person, an unidentified serial killer we have commonly called 'Jack the Ripper' for well over a century.

Referred to initially as the 'Whitechapel murderer' or 'Leather Apron' by members of the police force and the press alike, this mysterious figure's more famous moniker originated after George Lusk of the

Left: the infamous 'From Hell' letter ; Right: a front cover of an edition of the 'Police News'

Whitechapel Vigilance Committee received a written correspondence now commonly known as the 'From Hell' letter. Now widely considered a hoax - propagated, in all probability, by a person clever enough to imbue the letter with enough grammatical errors and grisly detail to suggest its author to be a deranged individual of limited intellect - the letter was accompanied by a small box containing half a human kidney, ostensibly an item that could have been easily acquired by a mischievous medical student fully appraised of the fact that Catherine Eddowes had been relieved of one of her kidneys by her killer. The letter read (as written, complete with errors) : 'From Hell. Mr Lusk, Sir. I send you half the kidne from one women prasarved it for you tother piece I fried and ate it was very nise. I may send you the bloody knif that I took it out if you only wate a whil longer. Jack the Ripper. Signed, Catch me when you can mishter Lusk.'

Up to 1891, the authorities had investigated a total of 11 murders in the area - collectively known as the Whitechapel murders (itself a misnomer, as a great many of the killings actually occurred in other London districts) - but it is the canonical five (Mary Ann Nichols, Annie Chapman, Elizabeth Stride, Catherine Eddowes and Mary Jane Kelly) committed between late August and early November of 1888 that have the most compelling evidence for being linked to the same person, each

Whitechapel, circa 1888

featuring the recurring deep throat slashes, abdominal and genital mutilations and body part removals generally associated with the ripper's modus operandi.

Over the intervening decades since these occurrences, many have attempted to work out the ripper's identity, and a combination of fact and folklore has gifted us a skewed and pseudo-historical modern view of the events and the Victorian world in which they happened. When we hear any mention of 'Jack the Ripper', our mind's eye instinctively conjures up a vision of some bonnet-adorned, gin-sodden whore or other, staggering out of a bawdy tavern and merrily making her way through fog-strewn, gas-lit alleyways, singing some colourful music-hall song of the day, before being mercilessly 'ripped' in some dark corner by a caped man wearing a high top hat and clutching a Gladstone bag. The cinema has played a considerable part in generating a stereotypical image of the murderer that has barely altered in decades, and Tempean's *Jack the Ripper* (1959) certainly added to that idea.

It is now widely accepted that the ripper strangled his victims before settling down to his gruesome work, but the Gladstone bag (a highly unlikely component of the killer's night-time inventory), has become part and parcel of our overall concept of the figure, along with the top hat and opera cape mentioned. This notion can be partially traced back to an article in *The Times* from October the 1st 1888 in which a certain Albert Bachert recalled drinking with a man in the Three Tuns Hotel in Aldgate who had asked him a succession of suspicious questions about the loose women of the area and their comings and goings. Bachert: 'He appeared to be a shabby genteel sort of man and was dressed in black clothes. He wore a black felt hat and carried a black bag.' In Tempean's film, the significance of this item is established by a comment uttered by a character who has witnessed a ripper attack, upon being questioned by the police: 'I didn't see 'im properly 'cause it was dark... But he was a posh fella. 'Ere, he was carrying a little black bag!'

Bachert (who succeeded George Lusk as head of the Whitechapel Vigilance Committee at some point in 1889), however, was a man with a penchant for self-publicity, desperate to insinuate himself into the ripper story as a figure of note, so much of what he is credited as having said in the many newspaper reports he featured in should probably be taken with a very large pinch of salt. Bachert was himself the recipient of a famous postcard - purportedly from the ripper - that mocked his blatant self-promotional tactics. Received on October the 20th 1888 and addressed to 'Mr Toby Baskett of 13 Newman Street, Whitechapel', the postcard read: 'Dear old Baskett, Yer only tried ter get yer name in the papers when yer thought you had me in the Three Tuns Hotel. I'd like to punch yer bleedin' nose. Jack the Ripper'

As serial killers go, Jack the Ripper has long endured as a fascinating but grisly enigma that still invites intense scrutiny to this day. The hypotheses that have arisen regarding his identity and motives are multi-fold, and the various theories regarding his nationality (the East-End area of London was subject to a huge influx of the Irish during the period, along with Tsarist Russians and Jewish immigrants of various origin) and the likelihood of his possessing medical expertise (or at least a basic surgical skill) are all well-documented.

For their 1959 offering, Baker and Berman drew upon the perhaps dubious claims held within a flawed but significant 1929 publication entitled *The Mystery of Jack the Ripper* for their source material. Written by the Australian-born journalist (and one-time UK Labour MP for Lambeth) Leonard Warburton Matters, the book puts forward the idea - based on an alleged (but completely unsubstantiated) deathbed confession - that the ripper's brutally violent acts were a series of revenge killings by a society doctor with a grudge against prostitutes - in particular, Mary Kelly - who, by the murderer's twisted logic, was guilty

Laird Cregar as *The Lodger* (1944)

of the death of his beloved son from syphilis. Post-mortem results on Kelly's remains rendered this theory unlikely, and the film itself excises this sordid detail from Matters' book in favour of an alternate plot in which the son instead commits suicide after he discovers that the love of his life (named Mary Clarke in the feature) is a harlot.

The ripper and his horrific acts had been portrayed on film on numerous occasions prior to 1959, albeit by characters who are fictional surrogates of the actual killer himself. Marie Belloc Lowndes' 1913 novel *The Lodger*, for instance, was adapted no less than four times up to '53 (Hitchcock's 1927 version starring Ivor Novello is possibly the most famous), and Hammer's *Room to Let* (1950) featured Valentine Dyall as escaped lunatic 'Dr Fell' in a tale highly reminiscent of these other pictures and patently derived from the same historical source. However, it was Tempean - in the subsidiary guise of Mid-Century Films - who finally released a picture that made no pretence about what, or who, it was portraying, as its title plainly proclaimed, despite the film's lack of historical accuracy. Baker: 'We were lucky to use the title, because the censor had banned the use of the title up until then. Many people had tried but the censor always turned it down. It so happened that we approached Trevelyan during a period when they were getting a little more relaxed on titles and even allowing a little more action in pictures, and some stuff you couldn't do before was now allowed.'

Once again, Jimmy Sangster was engaged by Baker and Berman to write the script from an original story outline presented to them by Peter

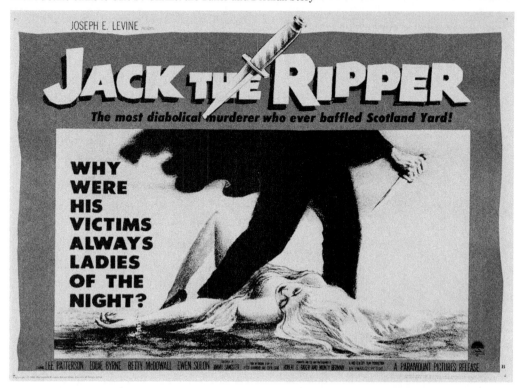

Hammond and Colin Craig. Now well-seasoned in churning out screenplays that delivered precisely what was required with apparent ease, Sangster produced a treatment unfettered by the troublesome stumbling block of historical fact, and profusely littered with all the clichéd and familiar details you would expect to find in a Victorian romp of this nature. After all, the tried and tested three-act construct that Sangster regularly employed to get the story told in an efficient manner did not allow for a wholly truthful depiction of events in a naturally unfolding time-frame and needed to be highly fictionalised in order to work. Sangster: 'I was always frightened that the truth would get in the way of the story. If the writer does his job properly then it feels right, and the audience doesn't notice.'

Sangster would soon find himself on very similar territory when he wrote the script for Hammer's thriller *The Man Who Could Cheat* Death (1959), adapted from the Barré Lyndon play *The Man in Half Moon Street*, a tale which contains many narrative parallels with the ripper case, such as the brutal murder of prostitutes and the removal of specific bodily parts. Between 1958 and 1960, it is safe to say that Sangster was dividing his creative output equally between Hammer (who he had worked for in various capacities from the days when they were known as Exclusive) and Tempean. *Jack the Ripper* was Sangster's third project for Baker and Berman, and there would be a handful more to come during the early part of the '60s.

The factual inaccuracies in the movie's depiction of events include a leading man character in the form of NYPD detective Sam Lowry - Lee Patterson of tv show *Surf-Side Six* fame (a Canadian, in fact), fulfilling the now seemingly obligatory 'token American' role - who, while conveniently on leave in foggy old London town (and sporting an oddly out-of-time 'Teddy-boy' hairstyle) offers

Denis Shaw as 'Simes'

to help the police, making head of the investigation Inspector O'Neill (Eddie Byrne) appear positively inept in the process. Detective Lowry is introduced early in proceedings when O'Neill is alerted by his desk sergeant to the presence of a visitor in the locality who has been heard asking questions about the ripper killings. The visitor is detective Lowry, and his line of enquiry in the 'Red Goose' public house has attracted the attention of an angry and suspicious mob of locals led by a portly ringleader named 'Simes' (*Curse of the Werewolf*'s Denis Shaw) who seems hell-bent on finding a scapegoat for the killings and accordingly encourages his accompanying rabble to attack this stranger. Simes: 'Come on then! What are you waiting for? They said the ripper was a foreigner!'

After the ugly atmosphere explodes into a briskly executed bar-room brawl, the violence is abruptly halted by the barmaid, who smashes a bottle over Simes' head before O'Neill arrives on the scene to restore order. Lowry is briefly taken with the pretty young barmaid (Anne Sharp as 'Helen') who has aided him, before he is taken outside and given the low-down on the effect the ripper killings are having on the locality. O'Neill: 'See for yourself... just look at this street. Before this ripper business started you could hardly move along here... stalls, barrel-organs, people spilling out of the pubs, it was a happy place. Not particularly moral, but happy.' Later, the barmaid becomes another victim of the ripper, killed while walking home alone, her mutilated body discovered by a drunk who has been thrown out of the local dance-hall as he staggers through the alleyways.

The film's plot is straightforward: The streets of London's Whitechapel

district are rife with fear and paranoia after a spate of killings of harlots and dance-hall girls. The local police seem impotent in their efforts to prevent further bloodshed, and subsequently a dangerous vigilante mentality festers among the locals, whose anger and frustration has primed them to attack anyone they mistrust or do not know, rather than rely on the police. Once detective Sam Lowry begins to aid Inspector O'Neill, it is not long before they ascertain that the murders are not just random acts of mindless violence, but a planned campaign designed to snuff out the life of a very specific prostitute. The investigative team's suspicion soon falls on the various staff of the 'Mercy Hospital for Women' as they strive to end the ripper's reign of terror and save the life of his ultimate victim, Mary Clarke.

To keep the audience guessing and maintain suspense, suspicion is drawn away from hospital governor Sir Rogers (the real villain of the piece) for as long as is required by a series of 'red herrings'; his fellow doctors Urquhart (Garard Green) and Tranter (John Le Mesurier) appear to act or look far more suspicious than he, attention is drawn to any male character in possession of a bag, and a completely different actor is used in the scenes where the ripper attacks his prey; the rasping voice of the ripper as he says to his various victims 'Mary Clarke? Are you Mary Clarke? Where can I find Mary Clarke?' even sounds like Le Mesurier as Tranter, to mislead even further. The character of Tranter makes various other potentially incriminating comments too, such as explaining his late arrival for a surgical procedure with the words 'Sorry

Dr Urquhart (Garard Green) and Anne Ford (Betty McDowall)

I'm late... outside case' and explaining during an operation that 'the secret of surgery these days' is 'to cut deeply'. Eventually, after stabbing his merry way through a succession of victims, 'Jack' finds Mary Clarke, and after explaining that he has been 'scouring the pavements so young men may be safe' he attacks her and leaves her to expire on her bed. Unfortunately for him, he clumsily leaves his bag behind, and it is soon recognised by Lowry as belonging to Rogers, leading to a confrontation at the hospital and the film's exciting climax.

The role of Sir David Rogers, the vengeful physicist with bloody murder on his mind was played by New Zealander Ewen Solon, who had only just appeared for Hammer in *The Hound of the Baskervilles* as the scheming 'Stapleton' when he was recruited to the cast. John Le Mesurier, who had already worked for Baker and Berman on *Blind Spot* and *Blood of the Vampire* the previous year, also made the direct leap from Hammer's adaptation of the Sherlock Holmes story - in which he played Sir Henry Baskerville's butler 'Barrymore' - into the frames of Tempean's new exercise in terror. Here, Le Mesurier's character of Dr Tranter disapproves strongly when detective Lowry develops an interest in Anne Ford (Betty McDowall), a feisty modern woman of whom he is the legal guardian.

McDowall does not have a great deal to do here, and I suspect that her presence in the film is purely a perfunctory one. Her character of Anne Ford is introduced via a contrived plot detail by which she is to temporarily take over the administrative position of 'lady almoner' (a sort of records clerk and receptionist) at the Mercy Hospital from a 'Mrs Bolton', but her main function seems to be to serve as additional 'eye-candy' (and love-interest of Detective Lowry), and as another potential endangered-female figure to be saved at some determined point in proceedings. Her participation also helps to endorse the film's intention of steering suspicion away from Sir David onto her guardian, as Dr Tranter often shows signs of having a controlling nature towards his ward, along with that stereotypical, overzealous Victorian attitude regarding the role of a woman in society that we have seen portrayed time and time again. Tranter is perplexed by what he describes as the 'disease of emancipation', leading us to believe that he may very well be harbouring a secret loathing for womankind and any semblance of female independence.

As with *Blood of the Vampire*, the villain of the piece is accompanied by an obligatory chamber-of-horrors style assistant in the form of Endre Muller's disfigured hunchback 'Louis Benz', who helps at the hospital with the instruments during surgical procedures and displays a certain amount of subdued menace. He is essentially another 'red herring' who is shown lurking in the shadows harbouring an apparent fascination with

Endre Muller as 'Louis'

the sharpness of the scalpels he is employed to handle. Also worthy of mention is (yet another!) Old Vic theatre veteran, George Rose, who plays the father of the ripper's intended victim, Mary Clarke. Rose would also appear in Tempean's next feature *The Flesh and the Fiends* as William Burke, in a far more substantial role that would properly display his abilities.

Funding the feature's £50,000 budget from a combination of National Film Finance Corporation money and pre-sales to distributor Regal Films, *Jack the Ripper* was shot on standing sets at Shepperton Studios, with Baker and Berman sharing the tasks of directing and cinematography. The pair did an excellent job, and the sequences where the ripper stalks his victims through the dimly lit streets before attacking them are deftly executed, with each killing given a greater effect by the simple but inspired technique of tilting the camera by an angle of 30 degrees, adding a jarring and psychotic aspect to proceedings. The design on the film is truly excellent, and the combination of the sets by art director William Kellner and costumes provided by Jack Verity provides a wonderful evocation of Victorian London and its various denizens.

Before they could begin production, of course, Baker and Berman would, as usual, need to submit their screenplay to the BBFC, and wait for its chairman John Trevelyan and his beady-eyed team of examiners to study the script and recommend any changes required for its approval. This would equally be the case with the finished picture's primary cut, which would prove to require several changes before being finally passed with an X-certificate.

In the meantime, the legendary American showman Joseph E. Levine of Embassy Pictures was more than happy to distribute the film, paying Baker and Berman £50,000 for the rights to a feature he was certain would be popular in the USA. Levine: 'I was merely fascinated with the quality of the piece and the manner in which it was produced... My sole thought upon acquiring the film was that here was the type of chiller the British do so very well. Mentally I catalogued it with such superb imported stage hits as *Ladies in Retirement*, *Angel Street* and *Dial M for Murder*.' This arrangement instantly covered the item's production costs, so Tempean were not too concerned with any temporary hold-ups with the BBFC.

Under the USA's far more relaxed MPAA ratings system, Levine was able to exhibit a version of *Jack the Ripper* far more in line with Baker and Berman's original vision, with some of the unsavoury elements vetoed by John Trevelyan and company intact. Additionally,

Producer Joseph E. Levine

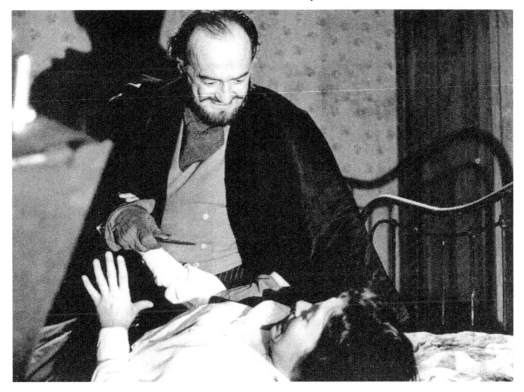

Sir David Rogers (Ewan Solon) attacks Mary Clarke (uncredited)

Levine shot a special prologue that included an opening narration by voice-over artist Paul Frees, and furthermore replaced the eerie original score rendered by Tempean regular composer Stanley Black with a more modern sounding, Jazz-tinged affair by Jimmy McHugh and Pete Rugolo. This may have ruffled Black's feathers a little, but it was not an usual practice: Baker: 'He (Levine) could do what he liked to it. Re-doing the music meant he could retain the publishing rights which are potentially worth a great deal of money. If you sell the film to a showman, you have to let him get on with it; he was going to do it anyway.' There was even a novelty 'Jack the Ripper' 45 rpm single released in the USA by RCA for promotional purposes, written by McHugh and Rugolo (in collaboration with Steve Allen) and sung by Nino Tempo.

Eventually, *Jack the Ripper* got its UK release on May 28, 1959, distributed by Regal Films. In the USA, it was released by Embassy Pictures (via Paramount) on February 17, 1960, preceded by an extravagant promotional campaign by Levine. At a special New York gala dinner for exhibitors that was attended by guests including the actor Peter Lorre and the burlesque entertainer Gypsy Rose Lee, Levine employed a brace of Brink's security guards to parade $1 million in cash before the astonished eyes of attendees, grandly announcing his intent to spend the entire sum on the film. Levine was known for such ostentatious behaviour, and indeed, he had imported and endorsed the Italian Peplum movie *Hercules* (made in 1958, distributed by Levine in '59) in much the same manner, with resounding success. However, despite claiming that his promotional expenditure on *Jack the Ripper* had resulted in a profit of $2 million, this was far less of a return than he had achieved on previous ventures and may well have been a face-saving exaggeration, in any case.

Furthermore, the item was boycotted in some areas such as Memphis, Tennessee and Manchester, New Hampshire, and critical response in the US was not as favourable as might have been hoped. *The New York Times* wrote: 'The most memorable line of dialogue in *Jack the Ripper* is read, appropriately enough, at an inquest. In the stentorian tones typical of the new Victorian melodrama, the coroner declaims that the police are "incompetent, inadequate and inept." He may have aimed his verdict at the law enforcers, but visitors to neighborhood theaters this week are likely to give his words a broader interpretation. That coroner would have made a good film critic.' Harsh words, but ones that hardly mattered to Baker and Berman. From their standpoint, *Jack the Ripper* was Tempean's most successful feature to date, and this factor would inform their decision to stay within the dark, criminal realms of the 19th century for their next gothic venture. It appeared that the company had - at least for a time - found its true calling, the cinematic reconstruction of certain distasteful historical events...

Chapter Five:

'This is the story of lost men and lost souls. It is a story of vice and murder. We make no apologies to the dead. It is all true.'

For their next feature *The Flesh and the Fiends* (1960), Tempean decided to focus on the terrible misdeeds of the infamous, Irish-born 'resurrection men' William Burke and William Hare, whose horrendous acts of grave-robbing and murder in the 1820s were committed at the behest of the Scottish anatomist Dr Robert Knox. On this occasion, Baker and Berman procured the directorial services of long-time associate John Gilling, who had an extensive amount of Tempean projects in his resume and had been involved with the company from its early days of producing 'quota quickies'. Gilling, who would also originate the screenplay for this newest picture, had a reputation for being difficult to work with, particularly in the case of female cast members (he had once upset Diana Dors on the 1951 film *The Quiet Woman* to such a point that she refused to continue working with him and had to be replaced) but Baker and Berman were keen for their picture to benefit from Gilling's strong visual sensibility and proven ability to orchestrate exciting action sequences. Baker: 'John was a very forceful director. He would upset people, but he

Artist's depiction of Burke and Hare

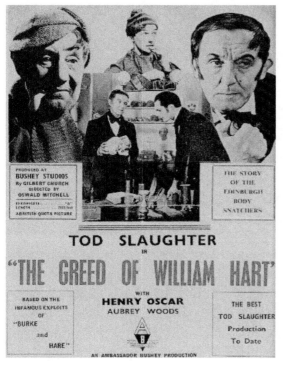

would get the job done. But he was an abrasive character, particularly with women.'

Gilling had already written a similar script - based on the exact same events as those which Baker and Berman now wished to recreate - in 1948, for the Tod Slaughter vehicle *The Greed of William Hart,* but had been prohibited by the BBFC on that occasion from using the real-life names of all those involved, substituting 'Burke and Hare' with 'Hart and Moore' and changing 'Dr Knox' to 'Dr Cox'. With Tempean's latest picture, Gilling was now able to freely use the correct names, although this freedom would not extend itself to the film's title. To further minimise any similarities between Gilling's earlier script and what would become known as *The Flesh and the Fiends* - and because Gilling was still under contract to Warwick Films with *Killers of Kilimanjaro* (1959) -

Leon Griffiths was brought on board to do a rewrite and polish of the original screenplay.

Griffiths was Sheffield born, but had been raised in Glasgow and was known to Tempean via his work writing for the television show *The Adventures of Robin Hood.* Both Gilling and Griffiths had been instructed to not over-embellish and to stay as close to the known facts as possible, to allow enough space for Baker and Berman to inject a little artistic license and copious amounts of salaciousness, violence and gore, all the while (as with *Jack the Ripper*) labouring under the pretence of rendering an historically accurate portrayal. For this enterprise, Baker,

Berman and Gilling conceived yet another subsidiary company, this time called Triad Productions. As with their previous film, Regal Films would handle the picture's distribution.

Much as before, the routine process ensued between Tempean and the BBFC, with John Trevelyan summoning Baker and Berman to his office to discuss several 'potentially offensive sequences' until both parties reached an agreement as to what was permissible, with the film eventually being passed with an X-certificate. Before shooting could commence though, Baker and Berman had one final obstacle to deal with. Executives at the Rank Organisation wanted to see Tempean's screenplay, as they themselves had a bodysnatching project languishing in their vaults and were concerned about a possible copyright infringement. After reading it, Rank fortunately returned it with their blessing and a customary 'good luck'. Incidentally, Rank's script (written by the Welsh poet Dylan Thomas, no less) remained unused for decades, until Mel Brooks acquired the rights to the screenplay and turned it (with Freddie Francis directing) into *The Doctor and the Devils* (1985) via his production company Brooksfilms.

The Flesh and the Fiends, like its predecessor, was filmed at Shepperton Studios, and - along with their later feature *The Siege of Sidney Street* - is one of Tempean's greatest achievements, a bona-fide British horror classic. Beautifully filmed in black and white, it certainly stands apart from everything else they produced before or after, for several reasons. Director Gilling, art director John Elphick and cinematographer Monty Berman managed to imbue the picture with a deliberately dark and unpleasant period flavour that reflects the grim and grimy nature of 19th century Edinburgh's 'old town' slum areas exceptionally well (a step up, even, from the admirable evocation of Victorian London rendered in *Jack the Ripper*).

However, the inventive team of Baker and Berman did occasionally improvise a little in their quest to get good results without spending too much cash, and to lend the film some additional panache 'on the cheap' they went as far as to delve into the Rank Organisation's library vaults for additional footage, buying crowd scenes originally created for David Lean's *Oliver Twist* (1948) and masterly blending this material with their own. *The Flesh and the Fiends* vividly displays the huge chasm that existed between the pitiful life then led by the very dregs of society and the more privileged existence enjoyed by the affluent members of Edinburgh's medical community, and it's unflinching depiction of the alarmingly quick descent of ordinary but desperate people into casual and brutal violence is shocking to see in a film of the period, with people remorselessly murdered in all manner of callous ways, their lives seemingly of little value in the grand scheme of things. What really makes the film so horrific, of course, is the fact that (as with *Jack the Ripper*) so much of what is portrayed is true. The greatest asset to the item, without doubt, is the exceptional cast of players whose sterling performances help raise it to a level above all of Baker and Berman's previous efforts. Most notable among these is Peter Cushing, whose acquisition would have been a real coup for Baker and Berman.

Cushing had spent the best part of two decades struggling towards becoming a household name, beginning his path towards a life less travelled in the 1930s, working and honing his skills in various English repertory companies before heading to Hollywood in a bid for stardom in 1938. Despite striking up friendships with such tinsel-town luminaries as Loretta Young, Carole Lombard and Louis Hayward (and his wife Ida Lupino); and landing small roles in several features - The Laurel and Hardy vehicle *A Chump at Oxford* (1939) and *Vigil in the Night* (1940) with Carole Lombard, among them - his dreams floundered, and he returned home to Britain in 1942, a sensitive man perhaps not meant for the cut-throat world of the Hollywood studio system, despite his gritty ambition.

From this point on, he worked tirelessly in the theatre throughout the remainder of the '40s (this included an Australasian tour with Laurence Olivier in 1948), until he finally made the transition to television in 1951 with the BBC production of JB Priestley's *Eden End*. His perseverance and years of hard work finally paid off when he won the *Daily Mail* Television Actor of the Year Award for 1953 after starring in television adaptations of Jane Austen's *Pride and Prejudice* and Eric Ambler's

Epitaph for a Spy. By the time Tempean acquired him for *The Flesh and the Fiends,* Cushing was a fully seasoned film actor and an extremely bankable asset, having just starred in an unbroken succession of roles in very successful Hammer movies that commenced with *The Curse of Frankenstein* (1957) and ran to *The Mummy* (1959).

In *Flesh and the Fiends*, Cushing plays the leading role of Dr Robert Knox, the skilled and flamboyant anatomist and fellow of the Royal Society of Edinburgh, a surgeon extraordinaire who

Cushing as 'Joseph Surface' in *School for Scandal* (1948)

enjoyed great popularity with a large contingent of students who would flock to his entertaining - and not for the squeamish - lectures on the human body held at John Barclay's anatomy school (of which he was a partner) in Surgeon's Square. Nowadays more notorious for his association with Burke and Hare, Knox's problems and descent into the world of grave-robbing (and murder, allegedly unknowingly) began when the legal provision of corpses, such as those of executed murderers, was failing to keep up with demand in a climate of huge interest in this new area of study, and an alternative way to obtain a regular supply of cadavers was required - which is where Burke and Hare came in.

Ultimately, the immoral and murderous methods by which Burke and Hare procured fresh specimens (they killed 16 people purely for monetary gain, in addition to any they may have taken from graves) was exposed, and they were arrested, along with Burke's wife Helen McDougal, who was thought to have aided them. At trial, Burke was found guilty and executed (later to be publicly dissected and his skeleton displayed, with a book made from his skin available to view at the police

Peter Cushing as the morally objectionable 'Dr Knox'

museum on Edinburgh's 'Royal Mile', even to this day) but Hare survived the hangman by turning King's evidence, and Burke's wife was also released without charge. Despite various fictionalised accounts to the contrary that tell us that he was blinded in some way by an angry mob, Hare disappeared into the ether, his eventual fate unknown. Knox himself was not prosecuted and was even exonerated by the Royal Society of Edinburgh on the grounds that he had not personally dealt with Burke and Hare, much to the outrage of local people (Knox's assistant David Paterson had apparently taken delivery of their grisly cargo).

Cushing's turn as Dr Knox is one of the most fascinating and complex roles of his career. Sporting a drooping left eyelid (as did the real-life Knox, who was blind in one eye and facially disfigured as a result of a bout of childhood smallpox), Cushing portrays Knox as a regal and dignified (but arrogant) man who has strayed from an ethical path through necessity and a burning desire to cut a swath through the ignorance and stupidity of the times in which he lived. Brilliantly intellectual but condescending and devoid of humour, Knox does not suffer fools gladly. With just a steely gaze or a scathing soliloquy of incisive wit, Knox is perfectly equipped to render those enemies on the medical council who do not agree with his ideas powerless to respond. Cushing, as Knox: 'If you would be so good as to incline your heads slightly to the right, you will observe the door. Please use it.'

In the film, Knox embodies a mind-set not dissimilar to that of Cushing's most famous horror characterisation, the Baron of Hammer's many 'Frankenstein' features, diffusing any moral dilemma over the real origins of his specimens by turning a blind eye (literally) to the methods possibly employed in their procurement, and, just like the Baron, Knox's opinion is that the end justifies the means; his pursuit of knowledge and scientific progression is for the ultimate benefit of mankind, so any objectionable acts performed in the service of that pursuit are therefore entirely justified. Cushing, as Knox: 'The individual is not important, emotion is a drug that dulls the senses.'

The film begins with a grim scene of two men digging up a body in a churchyard and hauling it away to their horse-drawn cart, before we are transported to the 'Academy of Dr Knox' in Edinburgh, where the renowned lecturer of anatomy is addressing a packed auditorium of his dedicated students, some of whom are about to graduate as fully qualified 'modern miracle-makers' after years of tutelage. Part of his teaching requires the dissection of the bodies of the dead, and due to the laws of the time Knox is finding the task of sourcing such specimens extremely difficult. Luckily, there is no shortage of desperate men willing to supply Knox with the materials he needs, exhuming the corpses of the newly departed, sometimes only hours after they have been interred.

Assigned to the job of receiving the illegal cadavers and paying grave-robbers what sometimes amounts to a small fortune (in the case of the freshest subjects) are Knox's assistant Dr Geoffrey Mitchell (Dermot Walsh) and an impressionable and naïve young student named Chris Jackson (former Rank player John Cairney) who is failing to graduate because he is, in Knox's words, 'far too emotional' and needs to 'approach the branch of medicine with a more clinical mind'.

After his lecture ends, Knox is surprised and delighted to find that his niece Martha (June Laverick) has returned home from France where she has spent several years in private tuition, now transformed from a 'gawky, long-legged schoolgirl' into a 'tribute to French cooking'. There is an obvious attraction between Martha and Knox's assistant Dr Mitchell, seen when Knox is called away to receive a body from grave-robber Rafael De La Torre ('Nice and fresh, Sir, just a week in the grave') and the pair are

left alone to recall their past acquaintance. Later, at local tavern 'The Merry Duke', the grave-robber and his companion drink away their ill-gotten gains in the company of prostitutes and are jealously observed by layabout drunkards Burke (George Rose, affecting a quite remarkable Tyrone / Donegal brogue) and Hare (Donald Pleasence), who are starting to think that perhaps they too should become resurrectionists, particularly seeing as Burke's wife has been pressurising him to look for work, a concept that is utterly abhorrent to him. While at the Merry Duke on an errand to pay the grave-robbers the balance of what they are owed, Knox's student Jackson makes the acquaintance of well-known local 'tart with a heart' Mary Patterson (Billie Whitelaw) after defending her against a drunken reveller.

Mary soon finds herself repaying the favour on the street outside when Jackson is set upon and clubbed to the ground by Burke and Hare, who have observed him with money in the tavern and are intent on relieving him of his funds. After being taken to her room to recover from his ordeal, Jackson is attracted to Mary and the pair kiss, initiating a romantic attachment. Despite her scandalous profession, Jackson is not perturbed in the least. On the contrary, he is unashamed to be seen in

public with Mary, and as time goes by a genuine and touching affection develops between the couple. Jackson: 'Mary... I'm proud of you. You know that... I'm the proudest man in the world.' Cairney (recollecting Whitelaw's concerns about just how far Gilling would go in their trysts): 'She did the scene with two plasters covering her nipples. They scratched my chest like razors and must have been murder to take off, but Billie told me "Otherwise my mother would be affronted".' In the meantime, we witness a similar bond forming between Dr Mitchell and Knox's niece Martha as they take a sunlit stroll along the riverbank, although this strand of the story has no great relevance and

merely serves to pad out the picture's running time. The trouble really begins when Burke and Hare return to Burke's house, where Burke's wife Helen (Renée Houston) informs him that one of their lodgers has 'passed away in the night without a word of warning', owing them three pounds in rent. Helen: 'Trust old John to take the easy way out!' It immediately occurs to Hare that they could profit by this tragic turn of events. Hare: 'You know, Burke, I was thinking. It's a shame for Johnny to be going to a pauper's grave, and him with an unpaid debt on his dying conscience. We could get six guineas for him up at the doctor's place and that would wipe out the debt!' Of course, once Burke and Hare realise just how easy it would be to earn money by supplying Knox with further specimens (and keep up a steady supply of liquor) they decide to approach their new career in a far more convenient manner than their grave-robbing counterparts and, proceeding with a twisted sense of entrepreneurialism, embark on a cold-hearted campaign of murder.

First to die at their cruel hands is drunken old woman Aggie (Esma Cannon, an actress adept at playing drunks, an ability she had exhibited previously in a minor role in *Jack the Ripper*), who they carry unseen from the Merry Duke to Burke's house, where, after a feeble protest from Helen, they continue to ply her with alcohol before she is suffocated by Burke, as Hare performs a macabre jig, dancing about with chilling jocularity. On receiving the wretched body of poor Aggie, Knox makes

Mary at the mercy of Hare after being lured back to Burke's house

only the briefest of half-hearted enquiries as to the nature of her demise before readily accepting her body, his lack of vigilance serving to spur Burke and Hare on to further atrocities. Hare: 'A man could become a millionaire at this game. Just think of it, Willie... Burke and Hare, members of the great medical profession!'

Despite the film's skilful way of offsetting the seriousness of Burke and Hare's dreadful exploits with moments of black humour and slapstick, several scenes are genuinely disturbing. Over time, Dr Mitchell and student Jackson begin to realise that the many bodies Burke and Hare are delivering to their premises may very well be victims of foul play. After a heated argument with Jackson, his sweetheart Mary storms out into the street into the waiting clutches of the deadly duo, who lure her back to Burke's house with the suggestion of a threesome where she is strangled by Hare. The moment when the love-struck Jackson discovers his own beloved's lifeless body laid out in the lecturing room is a deeply distressing one. Furthermore, when he seeks immediate vengeance and rashly confronts Burke and Hare, he himself is brutally stabbed to death

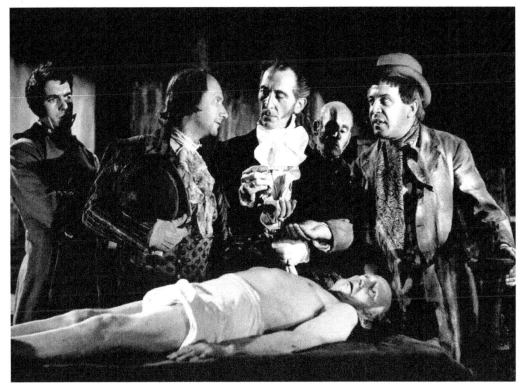

Burke and Hare deposit a body in the secret quarters of Knox's Academy

by an unhesitant Hare in an abrupt and casual manner that is both shocking and unexpected. Worst of all, though, is the heartless killing of a mentally impaired but well-loved local boy affectionately known in the area as 'daft Jamie' (Melvyn Hayes).

Clumsily throttled to death on the muddy floor of a pig pen after a desperate fight for his life, the terrified screams of the swine are the last thing poor Jamie ever hears, and it is this climactic murder that causes suspicion to finally fall on Burke and Hare, leading to their eventual capture by an angry mob of their peers. As in reality, Hare is set free

Melvyn Hayes as the ill-fated 'Daft Jamie'   **Swift justice is visited upon Hare**

(but has his eyes burned out by the enraged locals in this version of events) after turning King's Evidence against Burke, and Burke is duly hanged, complaining to the very end about not having been paid for the final body. Burke: 'If Knox had paid us for the subject like an honest man, I'd be standing here in a decent pair of trousers, meeting the public as I am for the first time.' Knox, as in life, is not prosecuted and continues to lecture, albeit with a sense of guilt, and is changed irrevocably after being awoken to the reality of the foul acts he himself has enabled. Knox, in a moment of candour with his devoted niece Martha: 'They (the murder victims) seemed so small in my scheme of things... but I knew how they died.'

As peripheral characters go, Dermot Walsh's 'Dr Mitchell' and John Cairney's 'Jackson' are serviceable enough, but the strongest and most memorable performances of all the film's cast - Peter Cushing aside - are provided by Donald Pleasence and Billie Whitelaw.

Born in Coventry in 1932, Whitelaw was a truly exceptional actress trained at RADA (the Royal Academy of Dramatic Art) who is perhaps best known for her 25-year-long association with the Irish playwright Samuel Beckett (whose work she was considered a foremost interpreter of), and her hypnotic, tour-de-force portrayal of nanny from Hell 'Mrs

A young Billie Whitelaw **Donald Pleasence in *From Beyond the Grave***

Baylock, acolyte of Satan and appointed guardian of the child Antichrist Damien Thorn in Richard Donner's 1976 classic supernatural thriller *The Omen*. As Mary Patterson, Whitelaw manages to beautifully exhibit the contrasting sides of her character, and whether playing Mary as a fiercely independent and tempestuous hard drinker or as a lonely and vulnerable woman willing to drop her guard and show her tender side to the right man, she is always eminently watchable. With this nuanced characterisation, Whitelaw manages to elicit a degree of sympathy for her character, making the terrible fate that befalls Mary Patterson that much harder to stomach.

Nottinghamshire-born actor Donald Pleasence (who also appeared

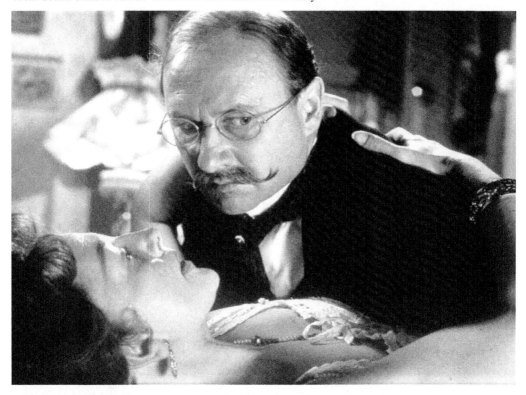

Donald Pleasence (pictured with Coral Browne) as *Dr Crippen* (1962)

with Billie Whitelaw in Hammer's 1960 crime thriller *Hell is a City*)
began his acting career in 1939, when he took up a position with the
Jersey Repertory Company before the outbreak of World War II brought
this pursuit to a temporary halt. Initially a conscientious objector,
Pleasence had a dramatic change of heart in the wake of the many
bombing raids visited upon London by the dreaded 'Luftwaffe', and
volunteered his services to the Royal Air Force, where he became a
wireless operator and took part in over sixty bombing raids against the
Axis powers. Pleasence was captured in 1944 after the Lancaster bomber
he was operating aboard was shot down during an attack on Agenville in
Northern France, and he spent the remainder of the war as a prisoner at
Stalag Luft I. After his release and discharge from the RAF in 1946, he
resumed acting and worked with repertory companies in Birmingham
and Bristol, but his rise to fame really began in the fifties, when - in
addition to his on-going theatre work - he garnered critical acclaim for
his portrayal of 'Syme' in Nigel Kneale's 1956 BBC adaptation of George
Orwell's dystopian novel *1984*.

A firm favourite among today's fans of horror and science-fiction
thanks to roles in the John Carpenter films *Halloween* (1978), *Escape*

from New York (1981) and *Prince of Darkness* (1987) - along with his participation in such British fare as *Death Line* (1972) and *From Beyond the Grave* (1974) - Pleasence was an actor with unusual but distinctive looks. Bald-headed and endowed with a penetrating stare and an intense, occasionally emotionless voice, Pleasence was an ideal candidate to play fanatical or unhinged villainous types steeped in the art of menace, and, despite enjoying an astonishingly varied career that spanned multiple genres and character types, these are the roles he is perhaps best remembered for; as exemplified by the films *Dr Crippen* (1962) - in which he played the titular real-life wife-murderer - and *You Only Live Twice* (1967), where he portrayed James Bond's arch-nemesis Ernst Stavro Blofeld, finally putting a face to the evil mastermind behind the SPECTRE organisation's many criminal endeavours. In *Flesh and the Fiends,* Pleasence practically steals the show as the sly and purely conscienceless psychopath William Hare. Receiving more actual screen time than lead actor Peter Cushing, Pleasence delivers a flesh-crawling performance that fills the heart and mind with dread and disgust. Like a bizarre feline in human form, Hare preens himself and slithers around odiously with an air of slippery perversion, garbed in his well-worn mountebank attire like a faded, down at heel dandy. Pleasence: 'George Rose and I were perfectly horrible grave-robbers. As I recall, that film had some rather bloody scenes which, in 1960, was a rare occurrence in horror films. That was an atmospheric film, and it portrayed the poverty of 19th century Europe realistically.'

For a feature apparently possessing all the pre-requisites for a box office success, the film only managed to achieve average returns, which must have been a disappointment for Baker and Berman. British critics seemed to recognise its merits, however, with *The Times* calling it 'a competent piece of work, concisely written with tension, dramatically sustained and well-acted' and *Time Out* concluding that it was 'much enlivened by the black-comic capering of Pleasence and Rose.' Its reviewer at *Film and Filming* magazine was marginally less impressed, stating that 'I can't understand anyone wishing to see this film voluntarily' but conceding that the production was 'technically, quite proficient.' Surprisingly, there were no initial offers to distribute the picture from America, but eventually it was afforded a small-scale US release in 1961 under the banner of the minor entity that was Valiant Films, being renamed to accentuate the film's horror overtones under the variable titles of *Mania* and *Psycho Killers,* only to ultimately perform

Allan Norwood's 'Flesh and the Fiends' novelisation from Corgi Books

poorly, despite *Variety*'s assessment of Peter Cushing's performance as a 'most effective study in single-minded integrity which knits the film together'.

Once again, a 'continental' variant of the version seen by UK audiences was created, this time containing more footage of bared flesh than ever before. Of the four gothic exercises generally collected under the umbrella term, this film and *Jack the* Ripper were the only true 'continental versions' made by Baker and Berman, simply because they featured the inclusion of scenes specifically re-shot to include gratuitous nudity, while the 'continental' variants of *Blood of the Vampire* and *The Hellfire Club* merely featured restored footage of scenes excised by the BBFC as they were deemed too shocking. In many ways, Tempean had reached a creative pinnacle with *The Flesh and the Fiends*, but paradoxically it was this very project that would plant seeds of doubt in the minds of Baker and Berman regarding the direction of their work, after an evident dip in public interest. Subsequently they would find themselves strongly reconsidering their position, proffering just one more similar entry before deciding to move on from gothic landscapes...

Chapter Six:

Chronologically, Baker and Berman's successive release to *The Flesh and the Fiends* was *The Siege of Sidney Street* (1960), but their next gothic-tinged item would be *The Hellfire Club*, a further sojourn into pseudo-historical territory that ultimately proved to be far less rooted in fact than either *Jack the Ripper* or *'Flesh'* and one of Tempean's weaker productions. The screenplay was the culmination of efforts by regular scribe Jimmy Sangster and relative newcomer Leon Griffiths, whose individual screenplays were scrutinised accordingly and moulded into an acceptable final treatment. Made on a modest budget between July and August of 1960 at Pinewood studios but released in early '61 under the 'New World' banner (with distribution again being handled by Regal), *The Hellfire Club* was co-directed by Baker and Berman themselves and photographed in Eastmancolor, a format which would once more evoke a 'Hammer-style' aesthetic that would serve in the picture's favour. The real-life Hellfire Club was an 18th century secret society (a belated successor to a previous, short-lived entity founded in 1719 by the Duke of Wharton) purportedly conceived by a certain Sir Francis Dashwood as an alternative to the dull, prescribed Sunday traditions he and his specially selected associates of influence and power had grown tired of.

Considering the society's legendary reputation for being a hotbed of

depravity, Tempean's 1961 feature had the potential, conceptually at least, to be both riotous and controversial. Unfortunately, what resulted on this occasion was a sumptuously staged but comparatively tame affair that would fail to deliver on the promise of its suggestive title and disappoint those expecting an overkill of salacious content. Co-writers Sangster and Griffiths could easily have conjured up a devilishly macabre tale littered with nubile bodies and derived from the skewed idea held by some that the club was a sinister assembly of Satanists with a sacrificial agenda, but instead they chose to weave a less ambitious and somewhat contrived tale of a young man (Keith Michell as 'Jason') and his struggle to regain his rightful title and inheritance following the death of his perverse father (*The Trollenberg Terror*'s Andrew Faulds as 'Lord Netherden'), whose estate he had fled from as a child some years before. Essentially a swashbuckling adventure yarn, the film is reasonably effective in this regard, but the Hellfire club depicted here serves simply as a backdrop to the story, a supposed den of iniquity only occasionally seen in the movie and with very little occurring within it of any real shock value.

The Hellfire Club does contain a small number of 'blink and you'll miss them' instances of mild nudity, however, such as the inclusion of a scene featuring lead actress Adrienne Corri luxuriating among the soap

Sir Francis Dashwood

suds in her ornate porcelain bath (her breasts fleetingly observed in a mirror), and another where the alluring German actress Kai Fischer returns to dry land after a swim in a reedy river and barely conceals her considerable charms behind the foliage of a bush. Sangster is reputed to have once jokingly described the film as a 'tits and swords' epic, and indeed, Adrienne Corri's finely sculptured figure, Kai Fischer's plunging neckline and ample bosom and the voluptuous curves of Caron Gardner - appearing uncredited as a 'speciality girl' in the latter part of the film - do provide brief moments of mild titillation. Hardly enough to warrant Sangster's overstated appraisal, though, and in fact, a review of the picture that appeared in a 1963 edition of the *New York Herald Tribune* said that 'what went on at the Hellfire would make Fanny Hill blush. The film merely plays up the club as a background... the orgies are strictly for grandma!' Presumably, Sangster could merely have been referring to the film's proclivity for showing as much cleavage and bare skin as it could get away with, while simultaneously teasing the audience with the promise of more. There are several moments which suggest that matters may well go further in this regard, such as a scene in the latter part of the movie where a lithe and elfin-like girl seductively belly-dances before an audience of cavorting decadents with nothing more than a pair of limpet shells to protect her modesty.

The tale of how the real-life Hellfire Club came into existence is an interesting one. Born into a life of privilege in London in 1708, its founder Francis Dashwood was educated at Eton college alongside future British prime minister William Pitt the Elder. Dashwood would himself become involved in politics as an adult, serving for many years as the parliamentary representative for New Romney and, in his later life, as Chancellor of the Exchequer; it appears that the moral duality of those in positions of power is nothing new. After his father's death in 1724,

Dashwood (then just 15 years old) inherited his father's estates and the baronetcies of West Wycombe and le Despencer. As a young man with untold wealth at his disposal, Dashwood travelled throughout Europe, becoming a figure of notoriety after allegedly impersonating Charles XII of Sweden with the sole intent of seducing Tsarina Anne of Russia and finding himself at one point expelled from the Papal states as a result of his questionable conduct. A little later in England, Dashwood became a prominent social figure, originating such fellowships as 'The Society of Dilettanti' (1734) - a club centred around the interests of classical art and fine dining and influenced by the culture experienced by Dashwood on his 'Grand Tour' travels through France, Germany, Italy and Denmark - and 'The Divan Club' (1744) which was dedicated to those with an interest in the Ottoman Empire.

The society which Dashwood is most famous for, of course - and the one most associated with this hell-raising English 'rake' is that byword in debauchery, the 'Hellfire Club', also known as the 'Monks of Medmenham Abbey' in honour of the remote Cistercian abbey that Dashwood renovated for the specific purpose of their meetings (the group would eventually relocate to the nearby 'Hellfire Caves', a network of flint and chalk caverns excavated by Dashwood himself). Inviting only those amongst his peers he considered to be of the right standing, Dashwood built up a brotherhood of refined men of a certain persuasion, broadminded individuals who would find within the confines of this 'gentlemen's club' a safe place to satiate their hedonistic pleasures, indulging in feasts of food and drink - accompanied by an assortment of female companions - and performing religious parodies and blasphemous rituals that praised pagan deities, all the while leading outwardly respectable lives of Christian hypocrisy. In Tempean's picture, there is no mention of Dashwood by name (in fact, each of the characters conjured up by Sangster and Griffiths are deliberately fictitious) but dramatic figures based loosely on the club's founder are featured, such as Lord Netherden (seen during the film's prologue) and the main villain of the piece, 'Thomas'.

Set during the reign of King George II, events begin in 1752 at the stately mansion of 'Netherden Hall', where libertine 'Hellfire Club' figurehead Lord Netherden is engaged in a mock sacrificial ceremony of a young woman, staged for the benefit of his assembled legion of decadent cronies. As the ceremony ends and Netherden's guests initiate an orgy, the spectacle is witnessed by the Lord's son Jason (portrayed as a child by *Village of the Damned*'s Martin Stephens) who has effectively been coerced into spying on his father by his wormy young cousin Thomas, who accompanies him. After being discovered at the scene by a drunken reveller, Jason is pursued by his enraged father and flees into the assumed safety of his mother's arms, while his sly cousin Thomas slinks away, undetected. Despite the protests of Lady Netherden (Jean Lodge, previously seen in Tempean's 1950 crime drama *Blackout*), Jason's father proclaims 'This is my house! He is my son and I shall do as I please!' before beating his son with a whip, much to the pleasure of cousin Thomas, who smiles gleefully and skulks in the background, his mission accomplished.

Concerned about her son's welfare and tired of her husband's controlling nature, Lady Netherden summons her coach driver Timothy (the prolific British character actor and comedy stalwart David Lodge) who is only too willing to help the lady and her son escape their perilous situation. Once on the road to London, Lady Netherden and son are pursued through the countryside by Lord Netherden and his lackies, who frantically race after their quarry on horseback. Suddenly, the coach lurches off the road, plunging down a grassy hill and crashing. Luckily, Jason has opted to ride upfront with the kindly Timothy, and both escape injury by hastily alighting the coach before impact. Witnessing the smashed wreckage, Lord Netherden barely registers concern, seeming almost pleased by the apparent death of his wife and child, before riding away. Jason realises his mother is mortally injured, and rushes to her side. Knowing her time is short, Lady Netherden implores Timothy to take her son far away. She then takes a locket from around her neck, passing it to Jason and urging him to 'return here only when you are old enough to combat "his" evil with kindness' before she dies.

Fifteen years pass by, and when we next see Jason (in the form of Keith Michell), he is a grown man and a member of a circus travelling through the Netherlands. After his faithful old friend Timothy receives news that Jason's father has died as the result of a hunting accident, the young man decides that he must leave his flame-haired sweetheart Yvonne (Kai Fischer) and fellow acrobat and companion Martin (Bill Owen), and return to England to claim his rightful title and make good on the promise made to his dying mother many years before. Jason is much loved by his circus companions, and, sad to see him depart, they bestow upon him the parting gift of a sword. Following advice from Timothy, Jason seeks out a slightly shady but enigmatic lawyer by the name of 'Merryweather' (Peter Cushing, in a guest star cameo) who may be able to help in his quest to regain his ancestral home. Once Jason locates Merryweather, he is warned by the attorney that proving his

identity is going to be difficult. On the assumption that he is dead, Jason's cousin Thomas, now himself grown to adulthood, has assumed the Lordship of Netherden along with the leadership of the Hellfire Club, positions he will no doubt be extremely reluctant to relinquish.

Presumably just as wickedly perverse as Jason's father had been, Thomas has managed to raise the organisation into being the de facto power behind the English throne, its membership profiteering from their various scurrilous schemes and the political influence they have mustered. In the firm belief that a letter exists somewhere in Netherden Hall that could prove the truth of Jason's heritage, Merryweather knowingly suggests to the young man that 'If one was dishonest, which of course, one is not, one could steal the letter. Especially if one knew one's way around Netherden Hall'. As Jason leaves the office, he notices a shifty looking clerk lurking in the corridor, apparently eavesdropping on the conversation. Peter Cushing - fresh from an excellent portrayal of the Sheriff of Nottingham in Hammer's 1960 Robin Hood feature *Sword of Sherwood Forest* - is typically reliable in the role of the snuff-inhaling Merryweather. With his overall screen time amounting to no more than ten minutes spread throughout the entire film, it is a shame that Cushing's contribution is so woefully brief, as he practically steals the show every time he appears.

Returning on horseback to the quaint and picturesque area where he

spent his childhood years, Jason finds the villagers of Netherden an unfriendly and wary bunch. Stopping at the local inn to enquire about lodgings, he sees a group of masked men - apparent members of the Hellfire Club - engaged in the persecution of a local man who has apparently affronted them, but Jason is powerless to help as the unfortunate villager is tied to the back of a horse and is mercilessly dragged across the ground as punishment. Later, as Jason rides around the countryside, he saves a beautiful and well-dressed young woman (Adrienne Corri as 'Isobel') from an attack by two vagabonds, fighting them off and displaying admirable physical prowess. This is witnessed by Isobel's suitor - and Jason's estranged cousin - Thomas (Peter Arne), who invites Jason (calling himself Caldwell) to dinner at Netherden Hall, believing at this point that the young man is a total stranger.

Accepting the invitation, Jason arrives at the mansion that evening, only to be ushered into the banqueting hall and subjected by Thomas to a tirade of humiliating insults purely for his own entertainment and that of a large group of assembled associates. Thomas then amuses himself further by promising Jason a 'job for life' if he can fight and defeat the burly coachman of his close friend Sir Hugh Manning (occasional Hammer star Francis Matthews, in a minor and forgettable role), much to Isobel's disapproval. Jason duly beats the coachman in combat but during the prolonged struggle he drops the locket given to him by his

beloved mother. Isobel, who by now has already developed a liking for Jason, picks up the item and returns it to him, but now harbours suspicions about his identity after recognising the locket as one featured in a portrait of Jason's mother that still hangs in the mansion's foyer.

As Isobel, Adrienne Corri (1930-2016) is as good as she possibly can be with the material presented to her and adds a considerable amount of class to the production, imbuing her character with a little of a real-life feistiness no doubt derived from her Lancastrian mother. Corri was an actress of great ability and presence who, over the years, enjoyed a certain degree of cult celebrity among film fans due to her involvement in such productions as *Corridors of Blood* (1958, with Boris Karloff and Christopher Lee - pictured above), the Compton-Tekli film *A Study in Terror* (1965), Stanley Kubrick's *A Clockwork Orange* (1971) and Hammer's *Vampire Circus* (1972). Her role of 'Mrs Alexander' in Kubrick's celebrated dystopian shocker is one of her most famous, a part that demonstrated her rigidly professional approach to her work - proved not only by her readiness to undergo the gruelling process of Kubrick's endless takes in his quest for perfection, but also by her willingness to bare every inch of her body without batting an eyelid. Corri (addressing co-star Malcolm McDowell): 'Well, Malcolm, you're about to find out that I'm a real redhead!'

Once in the employ of Thomas, Jason wastes no time in creeping into Netherden Hall, conveniently finding the letter he seeks with an implausible lack of difficulty. Finally, he has within his grasp the document that can prove he is the rightful Earl of Netherden. Unfortunately, it is here that the film begins to lose its way. Up to this point, the feature is reasonably compelling and believable, but from the halfway point on, our credulity is stretched immeasurably as the plot takes some ridiculous and bizarre turns and descends into near-farce. For reasons that cannot be fathomed, Jason's circus friends inexplicably abandon their tour through Europe to join him in England, along with his girlfriend Yvonne, who he welcomes gladly but with absolutely no mention of an earlier infidelity with Isobel, whose constant attempts to seduce him finally bear fruit. As unlikely as their visit seems, it is extremely fortunate that his friends turn up, as he soon finds himself badly in need of their help.

It transpires that the eavesdropping clerk outside Merryweather's office was a spy in the employ of Thomas, and it is not long before the usurper to the Earldom of Netherden knows the truth and sets his sights on disposing of Jason, sending his men to find and kill or capture him before he can fulfil his destiny. Peter Arne (a British actor whose life sadly ended prematurely in 1983 when he was bludgeoned to death in his

Peter Arne stars opposite Vincent Price in AIP's *The Oblong Box* (1969)

Knightsbridge flat by an unknown assailant) never really convinces in his role of Thomas, the evil villain of the piece. Despite his renown for such parts, here his performance seems one-noted and lacking the proper forcefulness and sense of dastardly wickedness required. However, his hateful vendetta against his estranged cousin does finally provide an opportunity for some much-needed action and a few situations of hero endangerment and 'derring-do'.

Australian actor Keith Michell - a familiar face to British television viewers of the early '70s thanks to his leading role in the popular BBC series *The Six Wives of Henry VIII* - is likeable and does his best to portray Jason as a brave and noble hero, but, as he makes narrow escapes from a variety of perilous situations his earnest endeavours are hindered by a brace of clumsily choreographed fight scenes, some unconvincing swordplay (both of which up the ante but lack spontaneity), the obvious use of stunt-doubles and at least one slightly speeded up chase sequence that results in a little unintentional mirth. Clifton Parker's lively and rousing score, however, fits perfectly and injects momentum and urgency into the action sequences. Parker - whose notable scores include *Treasure Island* (1950) and *Night of the Demon* (1957) - was a protégé of the prolific composer-conductor Muir Matheson, a pioneer of British film music. It is Matheson, in fact, who conducts the orchestra performing Parker's composition for this feature.

Eventually Thomas manages to capture Jason and gets him arrested on a trumped-up charge of murder. Tried at a courtroom presided over by a Judge played by Miles Malleson - a well-loved English actor who starred in such films as *Dead of Night* (1945), *Scrooge* (1951) and *The Brides of Dracula* (1960) - Jason is found guilty after false evidence is used against him and Merryweather fails to provide an adequate defence (a deliberate tactic by Cushing's wily lawyer to keep Jason safe from further attempts on his life), and is incarcerated at Newgate prison to await his execution. Of course, Jason escapes with the help of a band of his circus brethren which includes Adrienne Corri's future *Vampire Circus* co-star, the dwarf actor Skip Martin. Once free, Jason tracks down those who lied about him in court, getting them to retract their testimonies on pain of death and clearing his name. Merryweather then sets about getting the question of Jason's rightful title raised in the House of Lords.

The film's final scenes need to be seen to be believed, as Jason - now a free man and with his true love Yvonne now held captive by Thomas - infiltrates the Hellfire club's inner sanctum with the intention of rescuing her, disguised as one of Thomas's expected guests, an eccentric French Marquis whom he has managed to intercept before his arrival. Complete with powdered face, wig and false pointed beard, Jason gains entry to Netherden Hall and frees Yvonne, as *The Hellfire Club*'s last act morphs into a bizarre 'Scarlet Pimpernel' type scenario that is campily played for laughs but which eventually culminates in a deadly confrontation between hero and villain. Ultimately, this unusual and less inspiring addition to Tempean's admirable canon manages to overcome its shortcomings due to the efforts of its (mostly) impressive cast, its brisk pace and its decent production values, a peculiar instalment in Baker and Berman's resume that is essentially a piece of harmless, escapist whimsy that should not be taken too seriously. Audiences in the USA must have been even more perplexed than those in the UK upon witnessing the transatlantic version of the feature, which was drastically cut to just over an hour in length and released in America in a diminished black and white format. Baker and Berman produced a second swashbuckler in 1961 - also starring *The Hellfire Club*'s Peter Arne and Francis Matthews - titled *The Treasure of Monte Cristo* (US title: *The Secret of Monte Cristo*), an adaptation of an unofficial sequel to Alexandre Dumas' famous adventure novel *The Count of Monte Cristo*, before making an unexpected move into comedic territory with their final feature, *What a Carve Up!*...

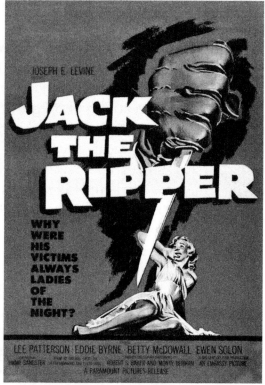

Chapter Seven:

As with any film being prepared for a UK cinema release, Tempean's features would have to go through the process of being rigidly scrutinised by the British Board of Film Censors (today known as the British Board of Film Classification). This non-governmental organisation was founded in 1912, its responsibilities including the examination of scripts at the pre-production stage to avoid morally objectionable subject matter, assessing what age restriction should be placed on any finished item placed before them, and deciding what was appropriate to include within the criteria of each classification, once established. With each of their four gothic features, Baker and Berman would find it necessary to make various changes to their projects to satisfy the requirements of the BBFC and its chairman John Trevelyan, and as a result the UK versions of these films would be the least objectionable of the various cuts that were rendered. Trevelyan, who had been an examiner for the BBFC since 1951, became its chairman and chief censor in '58, and from that point on had the final say in what material would survive the censorship process. He was generally regarded to have had a more liberal approach than some of his predecessors but could also be quite unpredictable in his decisions.

Despite Trevelyan's own credited assertion that censors were 'paid to have dirty minds', director Roy Ward Baker - who found his work subject to Trevelyan's scrutiny on numerous occasions with such Hammer entries as *The Vampire Lovers* (1970) and *Dr Jekyll and Sister Hyde*

John Trevelyan

(1971) - once said that 'Trevelyan had that schoolmasterly habit of pigeon-holing people. If you were in the box marked 'art cinema' you could tackle anything, however controversial: sex, violence, politics, religion - anything. If you were in 'commercial cinema' you faced obstruction and nit-picking all the way. He chose these categories and allocated everyone according to his estimation of them. He was a sinister, mean hypocrite, treating his favourites with nauseating unctuousness.' Baker and Berman were more than equipped to deal with Trevelyan, however, and when submitting scripts for the BBFC's perusal, they often applied a clever strategy. Baker: 'We would put a few dummy things in the films knowing he wouldn't let them through. If there were half-a-dozen things in the film he objected to, we would agree to take three out providing he let three stay in.' For the US releases, Baker and Berman could get away with a little more due to the far more relaxed MPAA ratings system, and in continental Europe it was possible to go even further, although by today's standards even the most explicit cuts of Tempean's gothic features seem relatively mild.

On examining the primary cut of *Blood of the Vampire,* the BBFC insisted on the following alterations: a small reduction to the opening scene where Callistratus (Donald Wolfit) is staked on the mountain-top, and a similar reduction to a scene  where an unfortunate inmate of the prison has a needle-tipped tube inserted into his neck as he cries out in anguish, his blood briefly spurting before it drains into a jar. Also absent from the UK print but restored in the European are the following: a grim and morbid establishing shot where the camera pans across a table in the laboratory, upon which are various items of glassware containing a decapitated head, dismembered body parts, internal organs and skull parts; an extremely short fragment of Carl's death scene where, after he is shot by the prison guards as he attempts to throw the lever that will free the Dobermanns, blood issues forth from his mouth and dribbles down his chin - there is a cut just before this occurs in the British version. Finally, there is the most considerable edit to the film of all, the notorious 'dungeon scene', which again features the hunchback Carl (Victor Maddern).

In the UK print, we simply see Carl strapping a girl (a housekeeper played by Barbara Burke) to a table in readiness for Dr Callistratus, but in the continental version we are shown exactly how she gets there. In the process of selecting the eventual victim, Carl skulks past a gallery of beautiful and voluptuous girls who are manacled to the dungeon wall. As

he does so, he ogles their ample chests, which are prominently displayed due to their flimsy, revealing garments. Reaching the third girl, he buries his face in her heaving bosom as the others look on in disgust and terror, before he finally moves on and selects the fourth, rendering her unconscious with a dab of chloroform before carrying her to the table. Of the various DVD releases of the title over recent years, the most complete version of the continental cut currently available is the French region 2 release from Artus, which includes the option of an English soundtrack. Of course, the European version of *Blood of the Vampire* was merely an alternate edit that restored footage deemed too unsavoury by the BBFC for UK audiences, but *Jack the Ripper*'s European variant would make the distinction of genuinely being 'continental' by including specially shot, more explicit alternate versions of scenes already present in the British cut. This would also be the case with *The Flesh and the Fiends*.

The first draft of Jimmy Sangster's *Jack the Ripper* script was submitted to the BBFC in December of 1957, but it was not well-received. The brutally executed killings and titillating can-can dancers found within its pages led to it being described by its assessor as 'a monstrous script, too full of sordid and sadistic association to be acceptable'. A revision of the script submitted in July 1958 also failed to get the green light, and Baker and Berman were summoned by John Trevelyan to the BBFC's London headquarters in Soho Square to discuss matters; during this meeting the producers agreed not only to film the picture in black and white but to also keep the various violent murders off-screen 'without unpleasant shots and close-ups of knives and victim's faces.' The problems did not end there, either, and when the finished item was submitted in February of 1959 the BBFC were once again unhappy with certain scenes that featured what they considered to be unnecessary and gratuitous violence, or naked breasts and such. It took many more months of negotiation and compromise before the film was finally passed for UK exhibition with an X certificate.

The British, American and European cuts of *Jack the Ripper* all differ from each other. In the US and European versions (but not in the UK edit) there is a small difference in the film's opening scene. After the ripper thrusts his knife into the stomach of an inebriated prostitute (Marianne Stone) we witness a shudder-inducing close-up of the knife being slowly withdrawn before being thrust into the victim's abdomen for a second time, the killer then gathering up his belongings and disappearing into the darkness like a phantom. In the British cut, there is only the first initial thrust. At the picture's climax, when the villainous Sir Rogers (Ewen Solon) is crushed to death beneath a descending lift, the American version of the film shows his blood seeping upwards through the floorboards, in 'technicolour'. This momentary colour rendering was an example of a short-lived fad that was prevalent at the time, also seen in AIP's *I Was a Teenage Frankenstein* (1958) and William Castle's *The Tingler* (1959). The seeping blood is not included in the UK print, but does appear in the continental, although not in colour.

The specially shot scenes only present in the continental cut all appear in a section of the film where Detective Lowry (Lee Patterson) visits the local dance-hall with his prospective sweetheart Anne (Betty McDowall), where they watch a troupe of dancing girls performing the 'can-can'. Among the audience with them are two well-heeled types - one of which is played by regular Hammer actor George Woodbridge (*Dracula, Revenge of Frankenstein, The Mummy*) - both of whom appear to be regular patrons of the establishment and partial to requesting the private company of various members of the chorus-line, a demand that the dance-hall's manager (Philip Leaver) is only too happy to accommodate. On this occasion, they select a pretty newcomer to the dance-hall by the name of Hazel (Jane Taylor), along with another dancer she has befriended, the kindly Maggie (Dorinda Stevens). It is at this point that the alternate footage appears...

As Hazel and Margaret retire to the communal dressing room to prepare themselves for their lurid assignation, several of the dancing girls are seen sat at their make-up tables in various stages of undress, many with their busts exposed. Suddenly, one of the dancers begins to

make derogatory remarks to Hazel, upon which Maggie springs to her defence and a fight breaks out. As Maggie struggles on the floor with her opponent, a handful of girls gather around to watch the spectacle, their breasts exposed and plainly displayed. The fight ends, and Hazel and Maggie join the men that have requested their company, and it is here that we have another short instance of partial nudity. As the girls entertain their guests, Maggie's male companion pours champagne over her chest, and in order to clean her dress, Maggie exposes one of her breasts.

The naïve and inexperienced Hazel cannot bring herself to go through with the charade, and, after her client tears the front of her dress, she storms out of the club, her hand holding her damaged clothing in place. There then follows a sequence that features restored footage excised by the BBFC and exclusive to the continental edit. As Hazel makes her way

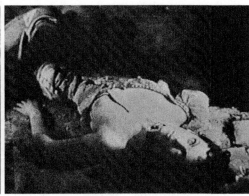

through the narrow streets, she chances upon the ripper, and, as she is attacked by the killer, the torn part of her dress falls away, uncovering one of her breasts. Later, when her corpse is discovered, Hazel is shown lying in the gutter with both breasts exposed (these two instances of nudity are replaced by clothed shots in all other prints). Anyone wishing to find this version of the movie should seek out the American 2-disc region 0 DVD release from Severin Films, which includes all three variants as well as several short documentary featurettes.

The continental version of *The Flesh and the Fiends* also features exclusive topless scenes, as well as restored footage cut by the BBFC. The footage not included in the UK print is as follows: during the murder of the drunken 'Aggie' (Esma Cannon) by Burke (George Rose), there are additional close-ups of Burke's hand as he smothers the old lady while Hare (Donald Pleasence) dances; the cruel killing of 'daft Jamie' (Melvyn Hayes) in the pig-pen is slightly extended and more violent. There is also a close-up of Burke's face as he is hanged at the end of the film. The topless takes only seen in the continental version are as follows: in the early scene where Burke and Hare are conversing in the 'Merry Duke' tavern, a female extra allows her blouse to slip and reveals her bust in the process; in a scene where Mary (Billie Whitelaw) leads her lover Jackson (John Cairney) up to her room, she stops at the foot of the stairs and converses with a woman who is stripped to the waist, her breasts exposed; there are also two scenes that take place in the brothel, both of which feature various extras engaged in topless revelry. The US region 0 DVD from Image Entertainment is recommended to those wanting to view the continental version of the film, as it is featured on their release, along with the original UK cut, the American *Fiendish Ghouls* trailer (its third truncated *US* release after the earlier *Mania* and *Psycho Killers*) and the alternate *Mania* opening title sequence.

Unfortunately, we can only imagine what excised and cut scenes feature in the continental variant of *The Hellfire Club*, as a full and unexpurgated version has yet to surface, but there certainly seems to be much in the film that could potentially have been 'sexed-up', what with the participation of the beautiful red-haired actresses Adrienne Corri and Kai Fischer, and the various featured 'speciality girls' such as Caron Gardner and Patricia Clapton. The practice of producing alternate films for a more liberal European market was unique to Tempean, an example of Baker and Berman's on-going adaptability and astute business sense. It has been suggested that Hammer followed Tempean's example, occasionally producing 'continental' versions of their own movies, but this is not strictly true. There may well be a legendary brief topless cutaway of Hazel Court in an elusive European print of 1959's *The Man Who Could Cheat Death* (apparently confirmed by the actress herself), but this can hardly be regarded as a sustained and deliberate practice in the same way as Baker and Berman's inspired approach demonstrated.

Chapter Eight:

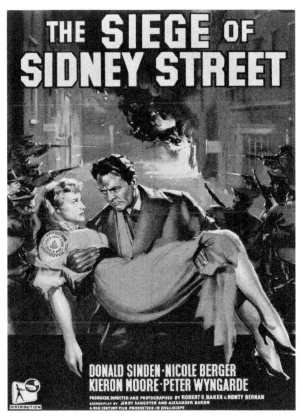

For Mid-Century Film's 1960 production *The Siege of Sidney Street*, Baker and Berman took as their next inspiration a sequence of real-life events that had come to a dramatic end just a few years before their respective birthdates, in the very area of London that Berman himself came from, the Whitechapel district. In the minds of some, the East-End of London is an area synonymous with criminal types and the unlawful schemes in which they embroil themselves, and although this ideal is largely a stereotypical one that has been perpetrated by decades of cinema and television dramas, it cannot be denied that the area does have a considerable legacy of notorious events, from the Ratcliffe Highway murders of 1811 through to the 'Jack the Ripper' killings of 1888 and the various unlawful acts attributed to the Kray twins during the 1960s. With *The Siege of Sidney Street*, Baker and Berman would bring to life another such famous East-End crime story, vividly wrought from yet another screenplay by Jimmy Sangster, this time written in collaboration with Alexander Baron (a future regular writer for television shows such as *Play for Today* and the original *Poldark*) and based on the events surrounding an infamous siege - also known as the Battle of Stepney - that occurred at 100 Sidney Street on January 3, 1911, when a combined force of policemen and soldiers cornered Fritz Szarrs and Josef Sokoloff, two Latvians who were holed up and armed with pistols on the second floor of the address.

The three victims of the Houndsditch incident   The scene of the Houndsditch incident

Suspects Peters, Gardstein, Svarrs and Dubov

Szarrs and Sokoloff were the last remaining members of a gang of dangerous and desperate anarchists calling themselves 'Leesma (Flame)'. This group, approximately thirteen strong in number - and counting female members among its ranks - had, over a period of time, been gradually and systematically brought to justice by the City of London and Metropolitan police forces for their involvement in a number of earlier crimes; namely a robbery of worker's wages at a rubber factory in North London now referred to as the 'Tottenham Outrage' that occurred in January 1909, and a further attempted robbery on December 16, 1910 - that of the Henry Harris jewellery store situated at 9 Exchange Buildings on the Houndsditch thoroughfare - a crime that resulted in the death of three officers from Bishopsgate police station (Sergeants Bentley and Tucker, Constable Choat) and the wounding of two more (Sergeant Bryant, Constable Woodham).

The 'Houndsditch Murders' as these killings are now known, remain to this day one of the worst instances of multiple murder of on-duty police officers in British history. Some modern historians have put forward the proposition that many of the shots fired on that fateful day came from the pistol of Yakov Peters, who was apprehended but evaded imprisonment

Yakov Peters as a young man

to become second in command of Cheka, the dreaded Bolshevik secret police force in post-revolutionary Russia, being acquitted along with two of his conspirators, Yourka Dubof and John Rosen at a trial held in May of 1911. A fourth perpetrator (Nina Vassileve) was convicted, although even this was later overturned on appeal. A fifth member called George Gardstein was shot during the police's attempts to apprehend the robbers and died later, being posthumously referred to during the trial as 'the Russian'. Despite being generally described as an anarchist movement, 'Leesma' were, to be more accurate, 'expropriators', individuals dedicated to a mutual cause whose criminal acts were committed purely to fund the Bolshevik party and its illustrious leader, Lenin.

The film begins very much as the real events of January 3rd did, with a policeman (a courageous Detective Sergeant by the name of Ben Leeson) making his way past the Coach and Horses public house through an early morning mist (around 7:30 am), eventually reaching his destination and throwing a pebble at a second floor window-pane before being shot down by one of the desperate inhabitants hiding inside 100 Sidney Street. The officer is followed at a distance by a stealthy company of fellow officers (in reality, none of these were married, a sure and telling indication of the grave and dangerous nature of the task before them), and as the shooting of Sergeant Leeson compels his colleagues to begin their assault on the house, the camera pans away to show a young woman at a nearby window, observing the drama that is unfolding in the street.

This is Sara (Nicole Berger), a girl seemingly under strict medical supervision, whose obvious distress indicates that she is in some way involved with the protagonists at 100 Sidney street. Berger was a Parisienne actress who tragically died in 1967 as the result of a car crash, killed as she was thrown from a car driven by friend Dany Dauberson,

a French singer famed for being France's entrant in the very first Eurovision song contest held in 1956. As the commotion continues out in the street, two nurses attempt to calm Sara down before a doctor administers a sedative to her, and as she succumbs to sleep, Sara's thoughts drift back to the past, to the day when she first met 'Peter'.

The story begins in earnest at a dance-hall where Sara works. A community of immigrants and locals are gathered together there, enjoying the spectacle of a Cossack dance and its lively accompanying folk-music. Sara, having finished her shift, makes her way through the merry throng, upon which she first encounters 'Peter' (Peter Wyngarde) who engages her in conversation before asking her to dance. At this point in his career, Wyngarde had just finished portraying Cyrano De Bergerac at the Bristol Old Vic (an engagement he personally considered a career highlight) and had also recently starred in an ITV adaptation of Julien Green's 1953 play 'South', a television drama generally considered the first ever to convey homosexual themes in an overt manner. As Wyngarde's 'Peter' acquaints himself with

The star-crossed lovers, Peter and Sara (Peter Wyngarde, Nicole Berger)

Sara on the dance-floor, a spectacled and nervous man enters the room and tells Peter that he has stolen a car. This is Dmitrieff (Tutte Lemkow), a member of a group to which Peter also belongs. It transpires that the group are planning a robbery (of the previously mentioned Tottenham rubber factory) and Dmitrieff is to be the getaway driver. Lemkow, who died in 1991, was of Jewish descent, a distinctively featured Norwegian actor who appeared in such notable productions as Hammer's *Stranglers of Bombay* (1959), *The Guns of Navarone* (1961) and *Fiddler on the Roof* (1971) during a long career in which he starred in over fifty feature films.

At the evening's end, Peter walks Sara to her lodgings, upon which she explains that she came to England from Europe after her family were killed by marauders who burned her village to the ground. After he bids her farewell, Peter then returns to a room which appears to be his group's headquarters, and we are introduced to his fellow members as they go through the details of their planned wages snatch. These include Toska (Kieron Moore), an unpleasant but self-assured man with a penchant for strumming a classical guitar and tormenting his sensitive and naïve young comrade Hefeld (James Caffrey). Further members include Lapidos (TP KcKenna), a female gang member by the name of Nina

Kieron Moore as 'Toska'   **James Caffrey as the troubled 'Hefeld'**

(Angela Newman) and her lover Gardstein (Maurice Good).

In real life, Gardstein was in all probability the real mastermind behind Leesma's crimes, and it is not even certain that Wyngarde's character existed at all. However, Sangster and Baron saw fit to bring to life the possibly mythical anarchist 'Peter the Painter' in their treatment, depicting him as a struggling artist and a romantic who has at some earlier undetermined point lost his own son to 'the cause'. Also among the group congregated in the group's meeting place is Svarrs, played by Leonard Sachs, a South African born British actor and 'old time music hall' enthusiast who is perhaps best known to British viewers for being the master of ceremonies on the long running BBC series *The Good Old Days*, a show on which he gained immense popularity for his elaborate and erudite introductions of the various performers who appeared on the show.

On the day of the gang's planned robbery, things do not go well. After two male employees of the 'London and District' bank arrive at the rubber factory to deliver worker's wages, Lapidos and Hefeld pounce on them and render them unconscious. Discovering that the bag containing the money is chained to one of the men's wrists, Lapidos shoots the chain to break it and the gunshot alerts the police. Although they successfully throw the cash over a wall to a waiting Toska as planned, Dmitrieff is unable to start the getaway car and subsequently fails to be at the

Nina, Gardstein and Svarrs - Angela Newman, Maurice Good, Leonard Sachs

rendezvous point to pick up Lapidos and Hefeld. The agents of law and order are quick to react, and before they have time to think Lapidos and Hefeld are being pursued across the open country by a task force headed by Inspectors Mannering (Donald Sinden) and Blakey (Godfrey Quigley).

Sinden - who in his later years became a stalwart of British television comedies such as *Two's Company* (1975-79; with Elaine Stritch) and *Never the Twain* (1981-1991; with Windsor Davies) - was, at the time of the film's making, contracted with the Rank Organisation and was one of the UK's prime box office favourites, having come to prominence in Ealing's *The Cruel Sea* (1953) and going on to appear in the recurrent role of the lecherous, under-achieving medical student 'Benskin' in the highly successful series of British 'Doctor' comedy movies. In his role as Inspector Mannering, Sinden delivers a typically dependable but unassuming performance, the kind he was known for and which had British housewives of the day voting him as 'the face we'd most like to see across our breakfast table'.

As the two robbers flee across the fields, Lapidos (who has twisted his ankle while climbing over railings) tells Hefeld that their only chance to escape is to split up, and the two make their separate ways towards different areas of a forest with the police in hot pursuit. Lapidos soon happens upon a cottage and tries to hide there, but Inspector Blakey soon finds him and shoots Lapidos dead when he refuses to surrender and threatens to harm an infant child. Hefeld eventually reaches a sprawling lake and begins to cross it, followed closely by a stray dog that has taken a liking to him and has been faithfully tailing him throughout the pursuit. Hiding behind a tree at the water's edge, Hefeld's location is given away by the barking dog, and realising he is only seconds away from capture, he decides to take his own life rather than submit to police interrogation.

Dmitrieff suffers a similar fate, after showing evidence of having lost his nerve and now regarded a liability by Peter, Toska and the others after failing to provide a mode of escape for Lapidos and Hefeld (Svarrs: 'Filth! Two men died for him!' - Toska: 'That little man will talk'). Dmitrieff is henceforth lured to a secluded area and, after pitifully pleading for his life ('I did my best, I couldn't help what happened with the car'), is routinely killed by a knife skilfully thrown by Toska. The stolen money - concealed in a basket and explained away as being political leaflets - is given by Nina to Sara, who is sworn to secrecy. Of course, by this point Sara is well on her way to being in love with Peter, and her complete trust in him ensures she does not question Nina's word. A romance soon blossoms between the two, but when Sara reads a newspaper headline regarding Dmitrieff's murder, her suspicions lead her to discover the stolen wages. Initially shocked, Peter soon placates her and justifies his actions by explaining that 'We steal because no-one will give... we steal so that there will never be any more refugees. So that people like your parents will not be massacred.' Furthermore, a firm friendship forms between Sara and Peter's female comrade Nina.

The Siege of Sidney Street was filmed at Ardmore Studios in Ireland, with exterior locations in the city of Dublin standing in for the pre-WWI streets of East London. Once again, Stanley Black provides the film's score, which includes a song entitled 'Ya Vas Lyu Blyu' (The Queen of Spades), an arrangement of Black's derived from a classical piece by Tchaikovsky, but here reinvented with the addition of lyrics written by David Palmer and Robert Musel. Once past its depiction of the 'Tottenham Outrage', the film's central section focuses on the subsequent Houndsditch incident. By the time we reach the final act, the criminal gang, as in real life, has been whittled down to a last few remaining members (Peter, Svarrs and Toska), and it is this trio that we see make a desperate stand against the police and the army laying siege to 100 Sidney Street during the movie's tense climax.

Overall, Jimmy Sangster and Alexander Baron's dramatization of the

Sara questions Peter about the stolen wages

events leading up to this final confrontation is reasonably faithful. During his younger days during the 1930s, Londoner Baron had been a leading activist and organiser of the Labour League of Youth (a group affiliated with the Communist Party of Great Britain) and had campaigned against fascists in the East End. Despite eventually becoming disillusioned with left-wing politics and breaking from the communists upon Stalin's 1939 pact with Adolf Hitler, Baron's background knowledge in this regard, in addition to his extensive

Alexander Baron

knowledge of East London's social underbelly (admirably demonstrated a few years later in his novel *The Lowlife* (1963) and its 1966 sequel *Strip Jack Naked*), would have been essential factors in helping endow Baker and Berman's depiction of events with at least a passing degree of believability.

In the aftermath of the film's depiction of the Houndsditch incident, the police become aware of just who they are dealing with and the danger they pose. With the remaining gang members gone to ground, known associate Nina (Angela Newman) is arrested and interrogated, but the police struggle to break her will, so they focus their attentions on Sara, who they have apprehended on the grounds that she has been seen with 'Peter the Painter' on several occasions. During this process, Sinden's Inspector Mannering realises the unwitting nature of Sara's involvement with the gang and develops a genuine fatherly affection for her after seeing the toll the whole situation has taken on her fragile emotions. However, Mannering's colleagues have other plans; to make use of Sara to flush out the gang, or at least discover their whereabouts. Nina is released from custody by the police, in the hope that she will reveal Peter's location to Sara, particularly after a 'dummy' newspaper is printed containing information they are convinced Nina will want to convey to her accomplices.

Inspector Mannering (Donald Sinden)

Sure enough, Nina visits Sara immediately upon release, and over the next day Nina and Sara are shadowed in their movements by the law, with Nina deliberately leading the police on a 'wild goose chase' by visiting places of little or no relevance. Mannering, however, tails Sara and she leads him to 100 Sidney Street. Making his way around the back of the house, Mannering climbs over the garden wall, removing his coat to place over the jagged stones that run along its top. Stealing into the property, Mannering is duly captured by Toska and taken to the room where Svarrs and Peter are hiding. Luckily, a local called 'Old Harry' (Harry Brogan) finds Mannering's coat, and, after he is picked up by the police, it is not long before they know the gang's location, leading to the film's exciting conclusion. Fortunately for Mannering, when Peter realises a police presence is mounting outside, he is surprisingly compelled by his love for Sara to let she and the Inspector go, before the inevitable siege begins.

To reiterate, the film's version of events is, for the most part, accurate, but for dramatic purposes Sangster and Baron seem to have used a liberal amount of artistic license in the crafting of their script in regard to the characters involved, presumably to deliver a suitably compact and effective narrative and to reduce the number of characters; Sangster had a track record with Baker and Berman in terms of stretching the truth in order to tell a concise and entertaining story, as had been the case with *Jack the Ripper* and *The Flesh and the Fiends*. In the event of *The Siege of Sidney Street* this proclivity of Sangster's is not quite as apparent, but it is most certainly there. For instance, there were in fact only two fugitives holed up in Sidney Street (Fritz Svarrs and Josef Sokoloff), but in the feature the lynch-pin character of Peter is added, and Sokoloff is substituted in the siege scenes (and throughout the entire picture, in fact) with Kieron Moore's deplorable character 'Toska'. Wyngarde's 'Peter the Painter', if he existed at all, was most certainly not present at the siege of Sidney Street.

Fritz Svarrs, as in life, is of course present in the tense final scenes, but is renamed 'Alex' in the feature for some reason. Also, there is a slight difference between the way the movie depicts the climax of the Tottenham incident and what truly transpired. In the film, Lapidos (TP McKenna) is shot and killed by Inspector Blakey (Godfrey Quigley) and Hefeld (James Caffrey) shoots himself, but in truth, Helfeld and Lepidus (the correct spelling of their names) both took their own lives rather than be captured. Further anomalies are apparent in the sequence that recalls the events of the failed jewellery theft at Houndsditch and the resultant murders. Svarrs (Leonard Sachs) and Toska are seen opening fire on the police as they attempt to evade capture. In fact, Svarrs and Sokoloff / Toska were not even present at Houndsditch, it was Gardstein and Yakov Peters, aided by their accomplices Yourka Dubof, Jon Rosen and Nina Vassileve.

The siege itself is very well re-enacted. The real siege was the first time in history that the London police had ever requested the aid of army personnel (a detachment of the Scots Guards, in fact) in a stand-off situation, which in this case persisted for around six hours. Despite heavily outnumbering their quarry, the police soon realised that their weapons were far inferior to those of Szarrs and Sokoloff, who also had far more ammunition than anyone could ever have expected. The shotguns supplied by a local gunsmith and used by many of the officers involved had limited range, and the Webley.450 revolvers used by several others had lingered unused in station arsenals for many years and were not in the best of working order.

Winston Churchill visits the scene of the siege

After several hours the then Home Secretary Winston Churchill sanctioned the added assistance of the Scots Guards, and once they arrived the situation was transformed, as their powerful rifle volleys caused so much damage to the second floor of the property that Svarrs and Sokoloff were forced to move down to the first and ground floors where they continued to shoot from the windows - controversially, Churchill even visited the battle scene at around noon, a reckless decision that could arguably have changed the entire course of British politics, if harm had befallen him. This visit is included in the film's enactment of events (though Churchill is referred to only as 'the Home Secretary'), and the famous figure is portrayed by an un-credited Jimmy Sangster, in his one and only acting credit.

The film makes an earnest attempt to replicate the weapons used by all those involved in the real-life events, at least within the limits of what they could acquire. In the feature, Webley .455 Mk IV revolvers are used by Inspectors Mannering and Blakely in place of the earlier .450 models really used by them, with 'Stevens' hammerless 'side by side' 12-gauge shotguns appearing in the movie which are practically identical to the type used by most of the uniformed officers who participated in the siege. As for the gang members, they are shown using Walther P38s in the picture. It has been established that, at least in relation to the crimes themselves, the following weapons were used. Svarrs and Gardstein favoured the German 7.63mm Mauser C96, Helfeld and Sokoloff used the 1910 FN Browning, Lepidus used an 1894 Bergman and Yakov Peters used a Dreyse pistol. A Mauser and FN Browning (a 1900 model) make brief appearances in the film, either being taken out of a kit bag or being aimed around a room, but do not feature in any of the main scenes. The Lee-Enfield No 1 Mk III rifle used by the Scots Guards at the siege are faithfully represented in the movie version.

By one o'clock in the afternoon of that fateful day, it was noticed that a fire had started inside 100 Sidney Street and the fire brigade was called, tasked not to extinguish the flames that were steadily burning up the house but simply to prevent the blaze from spreading to adjoining properties. It would now only be a matter of time before it would all be over for Szarrs and Sokoloff, and sure enough, by 2pm a combination of the Scots Guards' heavy and sustained rifle assault and the collapse of the house's infrastructure due to fire damage put an end to the fugitive's lives. As a result of this event's highlighting of the blatant ineffectuality of the Webley.450 revolver, the London police henceforth opted to use the superior Webley and Scott 32 calibre semi-automatic pistol. The fire that raged through the house is very well staged in the picture, and overall, *The Siege of Sydney Street* stands as Baker and Berman's most critically acclaimed work, and deservedly so.

Donald Sinden: 'The scene in the blazing room was filmed in the studio and I was vastly intrigued to watch the way the special effects people created the illusion. They began by making everything on the set completely fireproof. They then spread an inflammable jelly over the sections that were to be seen burning, and just before "Action" it was set alight. Tables and chairs and curtains blazed away and at the end of the scene the flames were extinguished ready for the next take. It was remarkable, nothing was damaged. Leonard Sachs who played Svarrs was left in the room with a revolver, his clothes had been fireproofed and in the long-shot flames licked from the jelly which had been put on his back. For the next shot, his close-up, he was having the jelly placed strategically on his shoulders and arms. I was talking to someone in the crew when another of the crew whispered to his colleague "Have they fireproofed his hair?" to which the reply was "No, I don't think they have, it would take twenty minutes." I was later informed that had Leonard suffered any damage, the insurance company would have paid up, but twenty minutes of the crew's time, on an hourly rate, merely to fireproof an actor's hair, would have had to have been paid for by the film company. Thankfully, Leonard only suffered mild burns to his hair and scalp!'

Chapter Nine:

Following on from their lavish, full-colour swashbucklers *The Hellfire Club* and *The Treasure of Monte Cristo*, Baker and Berman's final picture would see them return to the realms of terror - albeit with an infusion of humour - with the comedy-horror hybrid *What a Carve Up!* Released in 1961 (with the exclamation mark of its title added purely for extra emphasis), the production was helmed by former documentary maker and future television director Pat Jackson (with Monty Berman once again handling cinematography) and filmed at Twickenham Studios. The feature is a loose and jokey adaptation of Frank King's 1928 novel *The Ghoul* in which Jackson manages to achieve a fine balance of mild spookiness and laughs via a combination of quirky camera angles, competent cast performances and the atmospheric set designs of art director Ivan King. Frank King's book had already been adapted for the screen in 1933 by the Gaumont-British Picture Corporation, a straight telling of the tale that starred Boris Karloff (returning to his native England for the first time in over twenty years for its shooting) and directed by T Hayes Hunter, a director and producer who had primarily made his name during the 1920s making silent films for MGM.

Released under the New World Pictures banner and distributed once again by Regal, '*What a Carve Up!*' is essentially an 'old dark house' comedy variant that follows a storyline not dissimilar to that of John Willard's *The Cat and the Canary*, the 1922 stage play that has itself been adapted for the cinema screen on several occasions. Tempean's film was released in the USA the following year by *Jack the Ripper*'s distributor Joseph E. Levine (Embassy Pictures), but under the alternate title of *No Place Like Homicide*. The screenplay was co-written by comedy actors / writers Ray Cooney and Tony Hilton. Cooney began his career as a performer in various Brian Rix stage farces at London's Whitehall Theatre during the '50s, eventually

commencing a writing career of his own and becoming adept at crafting farces that were often infused with a typically British, bawdy humour that he favoured. Cooney's biggest success came in 1983 with the stage production *Run for Your Wife* (an adult comedy about the various misadventures of a bigamist London taxi cab-driver) which ran for nine consecutive years at various theatres in London's West End. The type of comedy that runs through Baker and Berman's last feature is of a somewhat vulgar nature, but fans of a certain kind of broad and earthy British humour not expecting anything too sophisticated will no doubt glean some degree of enjoyment out of Cooney and Hilton's rapid succession of risqué gags and double-entendres.

As in Willard's play, '*What a Carve Up!*' relates a now cliched and familiar narrative in which various estranged members of a squabbling family are summoned to a creepy and musty old mansion for the reading of a dead relative's will, all hoping to inherit a fortune but soon finding themselves targeted by a mysterious murderer intent on killing them all off, one by one. Following an opening credits sequence during which the overture of Muir Matheson's lively score uses a combination of themes both jaunty, playful and threatening to suggest the mixture of mirth and menace to follow, the picture begins with a proof-reader by the name of Ernie Broughton (Kenneth Connor) scaring himself witless as he peruses the pages of a paperback entitled 'The Fiend of the Second Floor

Flat', the spine of which oddly bears a completely different title ('The Second Pan Book of Horror Stories', in fact), the first of several noticeable blunders that occur throughout the movie that seem to have somehow escaped the attention of the continuity and editing team of Pamela Carlton and Gordon Pilkington.

Suddenly, as Ernie reads on and his imagination threatens to get the better of him, his flatmate - a bookmaker called 'Honest Syd Butler' (Sid James) - tumbles through the skylight into their kitchen, having climbed across the rooftops to gain entrance to the apartment because Ernie, embroiled in the terrifying details of his book, has failed to hear him ring the doorbell. After a brief debate regarding whose turn it is to make dinner, Syd reluctantly agrees to go to the 'fish and chippery' for 'double cod and chips' and duly leaves the flat to the sound of Ernie calling out 'don't forget the gherkins!' In Syd's absence, Ernie is visited by a sinister looking man who introduces himself as Everett Sloane, a solicitor (Donald Pleasence, in sombre black attire).

The creepy Sloane is the bearer of bad news, and, after removing his bowler hat, he solemnly informs Ernie that his uncle Gabriel has died from 'status lympathicus' (frightened to death, in other words!), and now nephew Ernie's presence is required - along with several other relatives - to attend the reading of the will, arranged to take place at the deceased's former residence Blackshaw Towers, an isolated country house situated in the lonely wilds of Yorkshire. On Syd's return, he encounters a departing Sloane on the stairs, and the comedic style generally employed in the feature is exemplified by the subsequent exchange between Syd and Ernie. After Syd asks him 'Who's that horrible looking zombie going down the stairs?' Ernie tells Syd that he is 'a beneficiary' to which Syd responds 'Filthy swine! How long can they give you for that?' Momentarily displaying faux concern for his uncle, it is not long before Ernie comes to his senses and returns to more pressing concerns, asking Syd 'Did you remember the gherkins?'

With hopes of personal financial gain in his crafty mind, Syd elects himself to the role of Ernie's 'legal advisor', and the hapless pair set off for Yorkshire. Arriving at the fictional train station of 'Workdale', the two

The real life location of Blackshaw Towers, Taplow Court

gather their belongings and make their way to Blackshaw Towers. As they negotiate their path across the treacherous, mist-strewn boggy moors that surround the estate, Ernie manages to clumsily consign Syd's suitcase (and his toothbrush) to the murky depths of the quagmire, much to Syd's annoyance. On arriving at the foreboding house - represented here by Taplow Court in Buckinghamshire, a mansion also seen in the 1962 horror movie *Night of the Eagle* (US title: *Burn, Witch, Burn*) - Ernie and Syd gain entrance by way of a front door that mysteriously opens of its own accord, before a black cat ominously crosses their paths and they gradually meet the other invited relatives.

The assembled guests include: Guy and Janet Broughton (Dennis Price and Valerie Taylor), who are Ernie's cousins; Dr Edward Broughton (George Woodbridge) who is Guy and Janet's father, brother of the deceased and Ernie's other uncle; Emily Broughton (Esma Cannon), an eccentric old lady mentally living in the past who is the aunt of Ernie, Guy and Janet and the sister of Edward and dead uncle Gabriel, and the organ playing Malcolm Broughton (Michael Gwynn), a man who professes that everyone is 'quite mad' and whose relationship to the others is, oddly, never established. Also present is Linda Dixon (Shirley Eaton), a pretty nurse responsible for Gabriel's healthcare prior to his death who Ernie takes an immediate shine to, and Gabriel's eerie old family retainer 'Fisk'. This limping, white-haired butler is played by Michael Gough (pre-dating his similar role of Bruce Wayne's butler

Fisk the Butler (Michael Gough)

Getting acquainted with Nurse Dickson

Alfred Pennyworth in Tim Burton's *Batman* (1989) and its sequels by nearly thirty years), a portrayal that seems to knowingly parody the often-overwrought acting style for which Gough is known - and sometimes derided - for.

With its use of innuendo and a cast that includes several 'Carry On' film regulars, the feature appears slightly like an unofficial entry in Peter Rogers' enduringly popular series. Up to 1961, five such movies had been made, and Kenneth Connor had starred in all of them, so his association with the series was well established and he was a familiar face to the public. Shirley Eaton had starred in three of the five, and at this point in her career was just a few years away from her most iconic screen role of Jill Masterson, the beautiful girl fated to die by skin suffocation after being literally painted to death by the eponymous villain of 1965's Bond thriller *Goldfinger*. Esma Cannon - an occasional Tempean star (and subject of one of *The Flesh and the Fiend*'s most chilling scenes) - had also starred in several of these early 'Carry On' entries, further enhancing this general impression.

Although he would also soon become synonymous with the franchise, Sid James(born in South Africa in 1913 as Solomon Joel Cohen) was at this point most famous for starring opposite Tony Hancock in Ray Galton and Alan Simpson's comedy *Hancock's Half Hour*, an association that began in 1954 with the radio version of the show and eventually ended in 1960 after six television series. At the time of starring in Baker and Berman's comedy, Sid James' screen persona had not quite developed into the one which would so endear him to his fans later, that of the mischievous but loveable rogue constantly in pursuit of a pretty girl, equipped with an irresistible cheeky grin and a highly recognisable and infectious laugh. In 1961 Sid James still retained the stocky build and bullish appearance that had enabled him to plausibly portray a variety of tough guy types in the many bit-parts and supporting roles he

Shirley Eaton between takes on Goldfinger'   **Sid James in Hammer's 'Quatermass 2 (1957)**

secured during the '50s, which incidentally included a turn as an Italian gangster in Tempean's very own *Escape by Night* (1953). James plays 'Honest Sid Butler' a little in this way, a wisecracking but no-nonsense individual with a wry expression and a shortness of patience, although his trademark chuckle does make an appearance here and there.

The drama progresses to the reading of the will, during which solicitor Sloane reveals to all that they have inherited nothing, except nurse Linda, who, much to her bemusement, has been left Gabriel's medicines and syringe, an expression of the deceased's warped sense of humour. Many of the relatives are incensed, apart from Aunty Emily, who just sits

knitting merrily in her own, muddled world. Suddenly, there is a power cut, so Ernie, Syd and Fisk go outside to the estate's generator to see if they can rectify the problem, only to find it has been sabotaged. On their return through the gathering darkness, they discover the body of Dr Broughton, sitting outside in a garden deckchair, apparently murdered. Syd attempts to alert

the police but finds that the lines have been mysteriously cut. With the remaining guests panic-stricken, stranded and suspecting each-other, Sloane recommends (insists, in fact) that they each lock themselves in their rooms and await the daylight.

Making his way upstairs, Ernie loses his way and blunders into Linda's room, where he is subjected to a tantalising glimpse of her physical form before making his excuses, despite his obvious affection for the nurse. Too nervous to spend the night alone, Ernie invites Syd to share his room, which is the very room in which uncle Gabriel purportedly died. After Ernie gives a nervous rendition of Sir Harry Lauder's romantic ditty 'Roamin' in the Gloamin' the pair settle down for the night but are kept awake by a mysterious 'tickler' beneath the bed-sheets. Ernie (sporting a comical night-cap) then realises that he needs to use the bathroom, and, while he is absent, a mysterious figure enters the room with the intention of stabbing Syd but misses his mark when his intended victim rolls over and murmurs in his sleep. This scene bears more than a passing resemblance to the classic 'haunted bedroom' routine featured in Hal Roach's MGM 3-reeler *The Laurel and Hardy Murder Case* (1930).

On his wanderings, Ernie enters the music room and starts playing 'Chopsticks' on the organ, upon which Malcolm appears and sits alongside him to join him in playing a duet. Suddenly, Malcolm is stabbed in the back, and Ernie screams in fright, alerting the others. Sloane discovers that the room was locked from within and casts his suspicion upon Ernie, before locking him in the music room along with Syd. However, Syd soon discovers a secret passage behind a rotating mirror, evidently the means by which the killer entered and alighted the murder scene. In the main lounge, nurse Linda complains to Sloane about his treatment of Ernie, protesting 'It's ridiculous! He wouldn't hurt a fly!', to which Sloane responds by remarking matter-of-factly that 'the young man's attitude towards insect life does not concern us, Miss Dickson.' Syd and Ernie then emerge from behind a sliding bookcase to reveal their findings to their companions, and Ernie is exonerated.

For safety's sake, everyone agrees to stay together in the lounge, but

this does not save Janet, who is killed by a poisonous dart (Sloane: 'Curare, the pygmy poison') that shoots out from behind a portrait of Gabriel. With Fisk the butler being the only person absent, they immediately suspect him, but he provides a suitable '5-minute-alibi' in the form of a cigarette almost smoked to completion with its extended ash-tip intact, proving his inactivity during the time of the murder. As the group confront Fisk in his below-stairs residence, he is seen sitting in his chair reading the novel *Lady Chatterley's Lover* by DH Lawrence, a timely reference to the prosecution of the book and its publisher Penguin Books under the Obscene Publication act that had been held at the Old Bailey courtroom the year before the film's making.

By now, both Emily and Ernie have reported seeing uncle Gabriel, which seems a total impossibility, seeing as he is apparently dead! An inspection of his coffin reveals it to be inhabited, but not by Gabriel, but by the murdered Malcolm. Sloane decides that enough is

enough and departs alone to alert the police in the local village. At this point, Guy (who has in his possession a small pistol) has disappeared. In due course, Inspector Arkwright (Philip O' Flynn) arrives at the house but is highly sceptical of the tale of faked death and homicide he is told, as the bodies of the various victims have inexplicably disappeared. Suddenly, a scream rings out, and Arkwright discovers the dead body of Guy, secreted inside a wall-mounted cocktail cabinet, his life extinguished. Meanwhile, Syd and Ernie discover Sloane dead in the fountain outside and realise with dismay that the solicitor could not possibly have sent the policeman, who it turns out is Gabriel Broughton in disguise, alive and with a deranged motive for murder in his heart.

Once discovered, Gabriel takes the rest of the group prisoner with the pistol acquired from Guy and explains that he is killing them all off for treating him badly and using him for his money. Locking his victims in a dungeon room and setting starving dogs onto them (mild echoes of *Blood of the Vampire*), Gabriel flees, cackling to himself.

Encountering Fisk, Gabriel attempts to shoot him but misses, triggering one of his own death traps in the process, and a chandelier drops onto him with fatal results. The imprisoned group, though trapped, are saved, as Fisk has earlier fed the dogs without Gabriel's knowledge and neutralised any danger they may have posed. At the film's end, when the survivors depart (each one, incidentally, a 'Carry On' participant), Ernie is left downhearted when he discovers that his prospective love Linda is already spoken for, as she is picked up from Blackshaw Towers by none other than Adam Faith, a popular singer and teen idol of the time, having scored big hits in the UK with such singles as 'What Do You Want (If You Don't Want Money)', 'Poor Me' and the festive release 'Lonely Pup (In a Christmas Shop).'

'What a Carve Up!' an interpretive artwork featuring characters from the film by Paul Draper

Chapter Ten:

By the early '60s, Robert Baker and Monty Berman - despite their incredible canon of work - were, in a commercial sense, just 'bubbling under'. However, their imagination and sense of purpose was about to lead them onto new ventures that would see them enjoy unprecedented success as the producers of a succession of cult television serials that would etch themselves into small-screen history and find a worldwide audience with the various characters whose adventures they would depict. The first of these projects was a televisual re-working of the stories written by Leslie Charteris that featured the character Simon Templar, otherwise known as 'The Saint'.

Simon Templar's alternate moniker of 'The Saint' is never fully explained in the books, other than as a nickname apparently given to him at the age of 19 by his peers and possibly derived from his initials. The character is most identifiable as a 'Robin Hood' style criminal, a debonair 'buccaneer in Saville Row attire' endowed with a boyish sense of humour and a habit of leaving his victims a calling card featuring a stick figure of a man with a halo above his head. In 1962, Charteris had been considering the possibility of a television deal for his series of books for quite some time but was fiercely protective of his creation and had

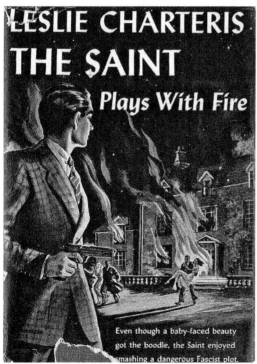

LESLIE CHARTERIS
THE SAINT
Plays With Fire

Even though a baby-faced beauty got the boodle, the Saint enjoyed smashing a dangerous Fascist plot.

turned many offers down flat, wary of letting Templar fall into the wrong hands. Charteris even asserted that the only Saint stories that could ever be adapted for the small screen would have to be written by himself. Charteris: 'I can be wrong about a lot of things; but on all matters concerning Simon Templar I can cheerfully proclaim myself to be the one and only infallible and incontrovertible expert on Earth, and this I shall continue to maintain, so help me.'

The Saint's adventures, of course, had already been adapted many times for the big screen. In 1938, when Charteris was working as a Hollywood screenwriter, he persuaded RKO pictures to produce a film based on his 1935

Author Leslie Charteris, and the iconic stick figure so synonymous with his 'Saint' character

novel *The Saint in New York*, starring Louis Hayward in the leading role, and between '38 and '43 a total of eight films were released, most featuring George Sanders as Templar. The third, *The Saint in London* (1939) was helmed by John Paddy Carstairs, and it was this director who helped to facilitate the character's televisual re-emergence. Carstairs was aware that Charteris was open to offers and recognised that Baker and Berman were ideal candidates. After a recommendation from Carstairs, Baker met with the author at his Florida residence, whereupon Charteris agreed, in principle, to allow them the rights for a series, although he still wanted creative control and an appropriate fee. Now Baker needed to find a company to fund production of an initial 26-episode series. Baker: 'Firstly, I took it to Associated-Rediffusion, but when I said that it would cost maybe £16,000 per episode, Brian Tessler turned it down. So, I went to ATV's Lew Grade, who jumped at it.'

Baker, as it turns out, already knew Grade (ATV was an ITV company run by the industry mogul, making programmes via its ITC sister subsidiary) and was aware of his instinct for a good project. Incredibly, Grade gave his approval within minutes of meeting Baker and, in a matter of days, Baker was flying back out to Florida to finalise the deal with Charteris and iron out the finer details. Grade, with his eye on the international markets, announced that the initial series would be shot on film rather than the cheaper 'telecine', a decision that would ramp up the cost to £30,000 an episode and give Charteris the required confidence in all concerned to relent on his insistence of having creative control of the project. Grade was firm in his belief that shooting the series on film would make *The Saint* appealing to the US market. Grade, in 1958: 'None but a fool makes television films for the British market alone. Without the guarantee of an American outlet he will lose his shirt.' Baker would acknowledge later that he thought Grade to be 'the greatest deal-maker in the world, the last of the great showmen', an assertion eventually vilified when *The Saint*'s six seasons (118 episodes made between 1962 and 1969) sold globally to more than 80 countries, realising a profit of over £350 million for ITC.

Grade had previously broken into the American market with the successful show *Danger Man* (US title: *Secret Agent*) starring Patrick McGoohan. Grade: 'There was a period of about six years when nobody in the USA wanted British TV programmes. It was really *Danger Man* that broke the bad run, and since then we have never looked back.' The job of sifting through the scores of stories written by Charteris and adapting them for television went to Harry Junkin, a Canadian story editor who had worked on the US soap opera *Love of Life* for many years. When it came to casting someone in the pivotal role of Simon Templar, Lew Grade's initial instinct was to suggest McGoohan for the part. Baker and Berman disagreed, however, and in any case McGoohan (a Catholic raised in New York by Irish emigrant parents) strongly disapproved of the Saint's promiscuous nature.

Instead, the part went to the 34-year old actor Roger Moore, who had been trained at RADA in his pre-war younger days, before working as a knitwear model in the early '50s, a job that earned him the nickname 'the big knit'. Following a few small parts on American television shows and several minor film roles while under contract to MGM, Moore's first real success as an actor came when he starred in 39 half-hour episodes of the UK children's television series *Ivanhoe* (1958-1959), before going on to star in the US Western serials *The Alaskans* (1959-1960) and *Maverick* (1960-61), both made by ABC / Warner Brothers. By the time Moore acquired the part of Simon Templar, his relaxed but enigmatic screen persona (complete with quizzical arched eyebrow) was fully formed, and his participation in *The Saint*, along with such elements as a

The legendary Lew Grade

Patrick McGoohan

Roger Moore in TV's 'Ivanhoe'

memorable theme-tune, the gimmick of an animated halo above its hero's head and Templar's signature Volvo P-1800 car made the show one of the most distinctive and popular of the '60s. For Moore's part, the success of the show had, by 1967, made him an international star and a household name with the world at his feet.

Roger Moore and Bob Baker during a break in filming

Moore as 'the Saint' in the iconic Volvo P-1800

Grade's faith in *The Saint*'s potential for being a US sensation was not rewarded immediately, however. Despite instant UK success and US syndication, the show did not properly make its mark in the States until 1966, when Lew Grade persuaded NBC executives to place it in a summertime slot left vacant by *The Dean Martin Show*, and the series began to gain popularity, with 47 brand new colour episodes being ordered by the network. Prior to this, Baker and Berman had answered a new demand for filmed television serials on the domestic front by supplying ITC with further shows for the ITV channel. *Gideon's Way* (1964-1966) - which followed the investigations of a Scotland Yard detective played by John Gregson - and *The Baron* (1966-1967) - a series starring Steve Forrest in the role of antiques dealer and undercover agent John Mannering - were both adapted from the books of John Creasey, an overlooked and often underappreciated author of detective and science-fiction stories who wrote over 600 novels using 28 different pseudonyms.

As the adventures of Simon Templar took off in the

United States, the long collaborative association of Baker and Berman came to an amicable end. Robert Baker entered into a new partnership with Roger Moore, and the pair formed their own production team called 'Barmore'. This was the company that would make the final 47 colour episodes of *The Saint* ordered by NBC, bringing those remaining stories by Charteris deemed worthy of adaptation by the producers to television screens on both sides of the Atlantic. Barmore also produced the 1969 film *Crossplot*, a 'swinging London' espionage thriller directed by Alvin Rakoff and starring Roger Moore as Gary Fenn, a talent scout for a modelling agency who becomes embroiled in the machinations of a shadowy organisation hell-bent on destabilising the existing world order and taking it over themselves. Considered by critics as nothing more than a dull and tedious, over-extended episode of *The Saint,* and lumbered with a convoluted and confusing plot, *Crossplot* is now considered by many as a dry-run for Roger Moore's ultimate career role of James Bond.

The character of Simon Templar would be reprised later with great success, of course, with *Return of the Saint,* a popular late '70s series starring occasional horror star Ian Ogilvy, who had appeared in *The Sorcerers* (1967 - with Boris Karloff, Susan George and Catherine Lacey), *Witchfinder General* (1968 - with Vincent Price, Patrick Wymark, Rupert Davies, Hilary Dwyer and Wilfred Brambell), *And Now the Screaming Starts!* (1973 - with Peter Cushing, Herbert Lom, Patrick Magee and Stephanie Beacham) and 'The Door' a segment of the Amicus portmanteau *From Beyond the Grave* (1974, with Leslie Anne-Down).

Ian Ogilvy with Boris Karloff in *The Sorcerers*   Ogilvy as Templar in *Return of the Saint*

Robert Baker was not only the executive producer on this follow-up series (which ran for just 24 episodes during 1978 and 1979) but also on the 1987 tv movie *The Saint in Manhattan* (with Andrew Clarke) and the big budget feature film that featured Val Kilmer as Simon Templar.

Once the original *Saint* came to its end and the 1970s dawned, Baker and Moore produced a second worldwide hit for ITC. Entitled *The Persuaders!* (1971-1972) this new series - which cost £100,000 per episode, a British budgetary record at the time - was pre-sold to the United States for £3m. Teaming Roger Moore with Tony Curtis (as Englishman Lord Brett Sinclair and American Danny Wilde respectively), the show featured the jet-setting adventures of two millionaire playboys acting as 'instruments of justice' for the retired Judge Fulton (Laurence Naismith) and apprehending errant criminals all around the globe at the Judge's behest. The idea for this new venture originated, incidentally, from one of the final episodes of its predecessor, a *Saint* adventure entitled 'The Ex-King of Diamonds' in which Simon Templar is partnered on a gambling escapade in Monte Carlo with a

Roger Moore stars in *The Persuaders!* with guest stars Joan Collins and Kirsten Lindholm

Texan oilman played by Stuart Damon (a later ITC star).

With each exciting instalment heralded in by John Barry's distinctive, synth-laden theme tune, the various episodes were enhanced each week by a veritable 'who's who' of recognisable guest stars such as Denholm Elliott, Terry-Thomas, Joss Ackland, Susan George, Kate O'Mara and Suzy Kendall to name but a few. Additionally, just as Simon Templar had his very own trademark car (the Volvo P-1800)', the protagonists of *The Persuaders!* were also afforded their very own distinctive signature

vehicles, with Brett Sinclair customarily driving a 'Bahama-Yellow' right-hand-drive 6-cylinder Aston Martin DBS with V8 wheels and markings, and Danny Wilde driving a red left-hand-drive Dino 246 GT.

However, despite the glamorous nature of this ambitious show and its assumed general appeal, *The Persuaders!* was not quite as popular in the US as had been anticipated, although it still did very well internationally, being dubbed into more than 20 languages (it was particularly popular in Australia and continental Europe). As series go, it was a short-lived affair, with just 26 episodes being made. Baker and Lew Grade decided to end production of the show when Roger Moore was offered - and accepted - the part of James Bond, following Sean Connery's 'final' relinquishment of the role (at least until his regrettable reprisal of the character for *Never Say Never Again* in 1983). Robert Baker states on the DVD documentary *The Morning After* that Lew Grade was prepared - despite the show's American failure - to finance a second series with Noel Harrison (son of Rex) in the place of Moore, but Baker dissuaded Grade, stating that the dynamic between the original two leads was so unique and strong that it was better to let the project finish on a high.

Looking back now, Moore's acceptance of the part of 007 seems like a no-brainer, but the apparent uneasy working relationship (it was publicly maintained that it was amicable) between himself and Tony Curtis could also have been a contributory factor. There has been much speculation about this matter over the years, with one-time *Persuaders!* guest-star Joan Collins asserting that Curtis was a man with a foul temper that created an often unbearably tense on-set atmosphere, and

Stars of *The Persuaders*! Roger Moore and Tony Curtis with Sir Lew Grade and Robert Baker

Roger Moore himself validated rumours of his co-star's prolific and casual use of cannabis. Val Guest (director): 'Tony was on pot at the time, and I used to have to say "Oh, go and have a smoke" because he always had some gripe of some kind. One day we were shooting on the Croisette in Cannes and we'd been roped off, with crowds all around us watching us film and everything, and Tony Curtis came down to do his scene and he was carrying on at the wardrobe people saying "You didn't do this, and you should have done that... and in Hollywood you would have been fired", and dear old Roger Moore walked over, took him by his lapels, looked him straight in the eyes and said "And to think those lips once kissed Piper Laurie". Well, the whole of the Croisette collapsed, the unit collapsed, and, I must say, even Tony had to laugh. We got the award that year for the best TV series, and they wanted us to do another, and I remember Roger saying "With Tony Curtis? Not on your life!"

Meanwhile, the equally capable Monty Berman, himself equipped with an intuitive ability to gauge public tastes and originate new concepts of his own, also continued to produce further tele-fantasy programmes for ITC from 1967 onwards, aided by the prolific writer and script editor Dennis Spooner, who he had met while Spooner was working on *The Baron*. The pair formed their own company called 'Scoton', their output of cult television culminating with *The Champions* (30 episodes; 1968-1969). With an opening sequence that featured a theme tune composed by British song-writing stalwart Tony Hatch (Petula Clark), *The Champions* follows the adventures of Richard Barrett (William Gaunt), Sharron Macready (Alexandra Bastedo) and Craig Stirling (Stuart

William Gaunt and Alexandra Bastedo as two of the super-powered '*Champions*'

Damon), members of a Geneva-based United Nations organisation called 'Nemesis'. After a plane crash in a mysterious region of the Himalayas, the three operatives are found by a secret Tibetan race who bestow upon them the powers of telepathy and precognition, which they use to battle against Nazi enemies and fascist regimes throughout the course of the series.

One noticeable difference between this new project from Berman and Spooner (and indeed, those that followed it) and the shows Baker and Moore made with Lew Grade was budget. In place of the genuine international locations and expensive-looking scenery that came from the healthy cash-supply afforded to *The Saint* and *The Persuaders*! were cheaper sets (some of which were used again and again on several different episodes), stock footage and exterior action sequences filmed in Borehamwood, near Elstree Studios. The series did, however, benefit from a healthy succession of guest-star appearances - from actors such as Donald Sutherland, Hannah Gordon, Burt Kwouk and Imogen Hassall - and from the participation of an assemblage of now highly celebrated cult television writers that included Brian Clemens, Terry Nation, Tony Williamson and Dennis Spooner himself.

Next for Berman and Spooner came *Randall and Hopkirk: Deceased* (US title: *My Partner the Ghost;* 26 episodes; 1969-1970), a series in which struggling private detective Jeff Randall (Mike Pratt) is aided in his investigations by the ghost of his dead partner Marty Hopkirk (Kenneth Cope, killed in the pilot episode by a hit-and-run driver but cursed to walk the land of the living for a hundred years after staying out of his grave just a little too long). Only Randall can see Hopkirk's spirit, and soon comes to realise that having his old friend around as an invisible companion could really help him to solve his various cases.

Spooner's concept for the show, which mixed elements of the paranormal with crime-drama, action and light comedy, was influenced by his love of such films as *Topper* (1937) and *Blithe Spirit* (1945) - which feature similar themes - and also by his avid interest in the supernatural. During the show's audition / screen-testing process, Berman and Spooner agreed that Mike Pratt and Kenneth Cope had suitable chemistry and cast them in their parts. The two actors were already known to Berman and Spooner in any case, as Pratt had previously appeared in *The Baron* and Cope had a resume of previous television work that included *The Avengers* and *Z Cars*. Australian actress Annette Andre completed the show's regular cast with her role of Marty's widow 'Jeannie', who just happens to be the secretary at Randall and Hopkirk's private detective agency.

As with *The Champions*, *Randall and Hopkirk: Deceased* was filmed on a restrictive budget, shot mainly on studio-bound sets and with very little location work. Exterior scenes, when they appeared, were usually simulated with the use of 'bluescreen'. Similarly, the effects of making

Hopkirk suddenly appear out of the ether or making his presence felt by those unable to see him were achieved using only the most basic of studio trickery. In line with other ITC serials, iconic cars were featured, (in this case the Vauxhall Victor 2000 FD and a red Austin Mini) and the show's theme-tune (a harpsichord and flute-driven affair reminiscent of *The Ipcress File*'s score) was composed by Edwin Astley, who had previously provided the themes for *Danger Man* and *The Saint*.

Shot back-to-back with *Randall and Hopkirk: Deceased* at Elstree - and utilising many of the same cast, crew, sets and even motor vehicles - *Department S* (28 episodes; 1969-1970) relayed the exploits of Jason King (Peter Wyngarde), Stewart Sullivan (Joel Fabiani) and Annabel Hurst (Rosemary Nichols), three members of a fictional strand of Interpol named in the show's title who work under the watchful eye of their boss Sir Curtis Seretse (Dennis Alaba Peters). In its follow-up series *Jason King* (26 episodes; 1971-1972), King is no longer working with Department S, but is an author of adventure novels with a flamboyant fashion sense and an eye for the ladies. The research he undertakes while writing his 'Mark Caine' series of novels seems to constantly draw him into situations where his investigative skills are required.

It can be justly asserted that Baker and Berman's various small-screen projects changed the face of television. These slickly produced, glossily presented and action-packed programmes ushered in a new era in which the previously stale and predictable schedules offered to the viewing public were shaken up considerably. The high production values of their many shows are a testament to Baker and Berman's craftmanship and commitment to quality, and their importance in the process of transforming the '60s and '70s into a Golden Age of British television should never be understated. In the guise of Tempean, Baker and Berman's substantial output of feature films stands as an equally impressive and inspired body of work, a cinematic legacy with an importance and relevance that will resonate for many decades to come.

IN MEMORIAM

After his final ITC series *The Adventurer* (26 episodes; 1972-1973, with Gene Barry), Berman retired from production but lived to see much of the work he created with Tempean and ITC given its proper dues, as a variety of these projects were revived during the video and satellite renaissance of the '90s and revealed to an appreciative new audience. After 34 puzzling years of reclusive life and silence, Nestor Montague 'Monty' Berman passed away aged 92 on June 14, 2006.

As previously mentioned, Baker, in the latter part of his career, was executive producer for *Return of the Saint*, the 1987 TV movie *The Saint in Manhattan* and the 1997 big budget feature film based on the Simon Templar character. He also devised the 1986 adventure serial *Return to Treasure Island* - a sequel of sorts to Robert Louis Stevenson's original novel - starring Brian Blessed as 'Long John Silver'. Robert Sidney Baker passed away aged 92 on September 30, 2009.

Printed in Great Britain
by Amazon